# OWLS COLORING BOOK FOR KIDS

## AGES 4-8

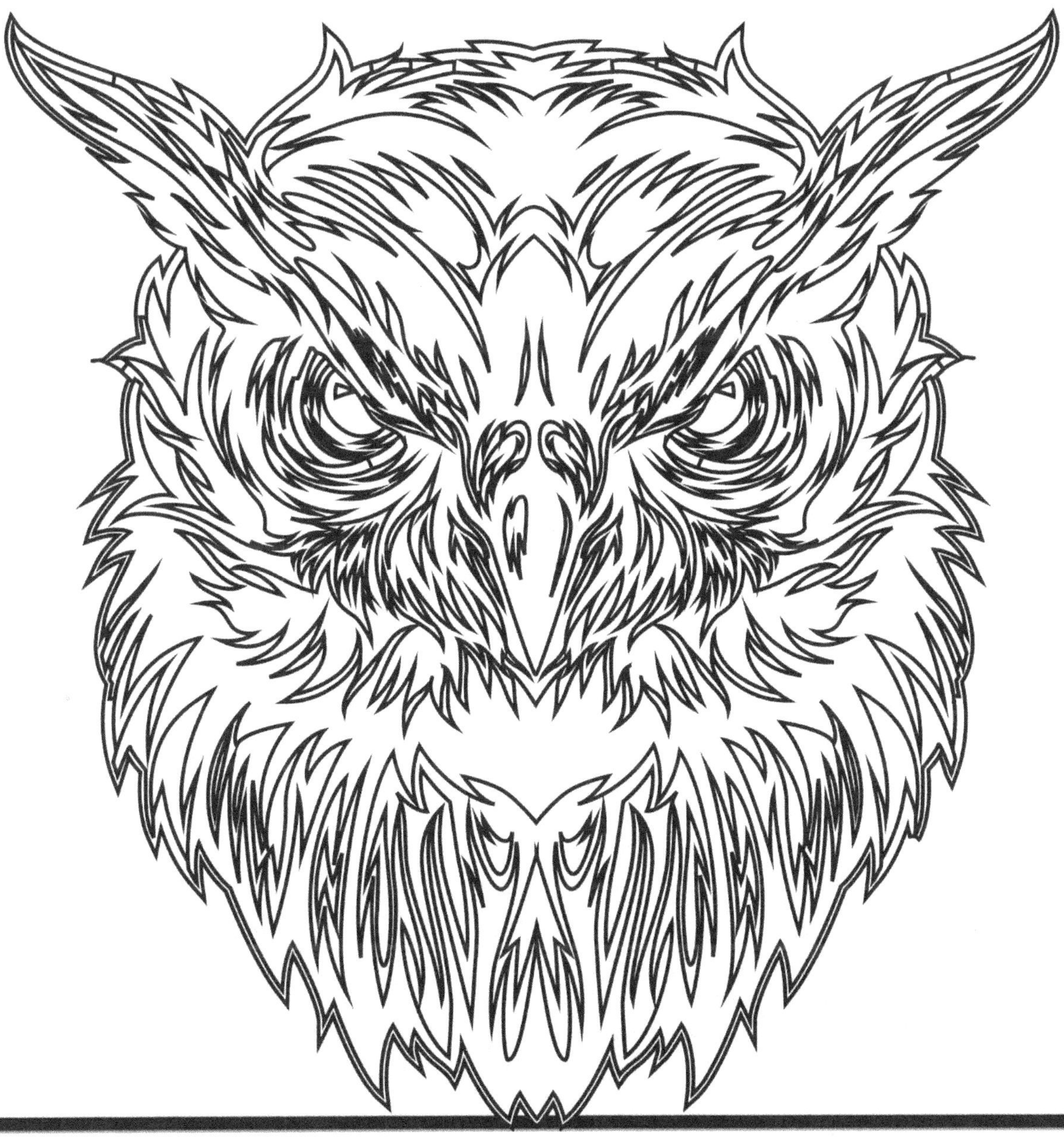

# THIS BOOK BELONG TO

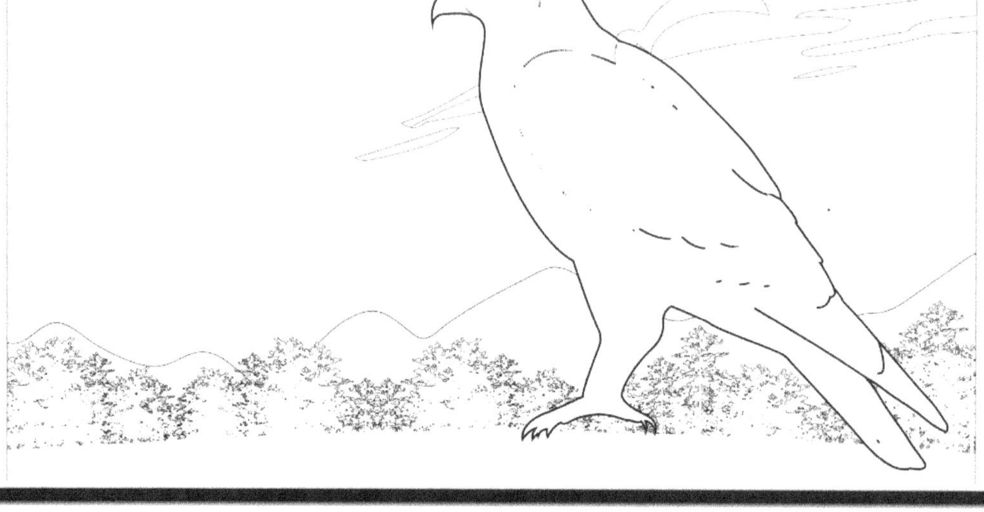

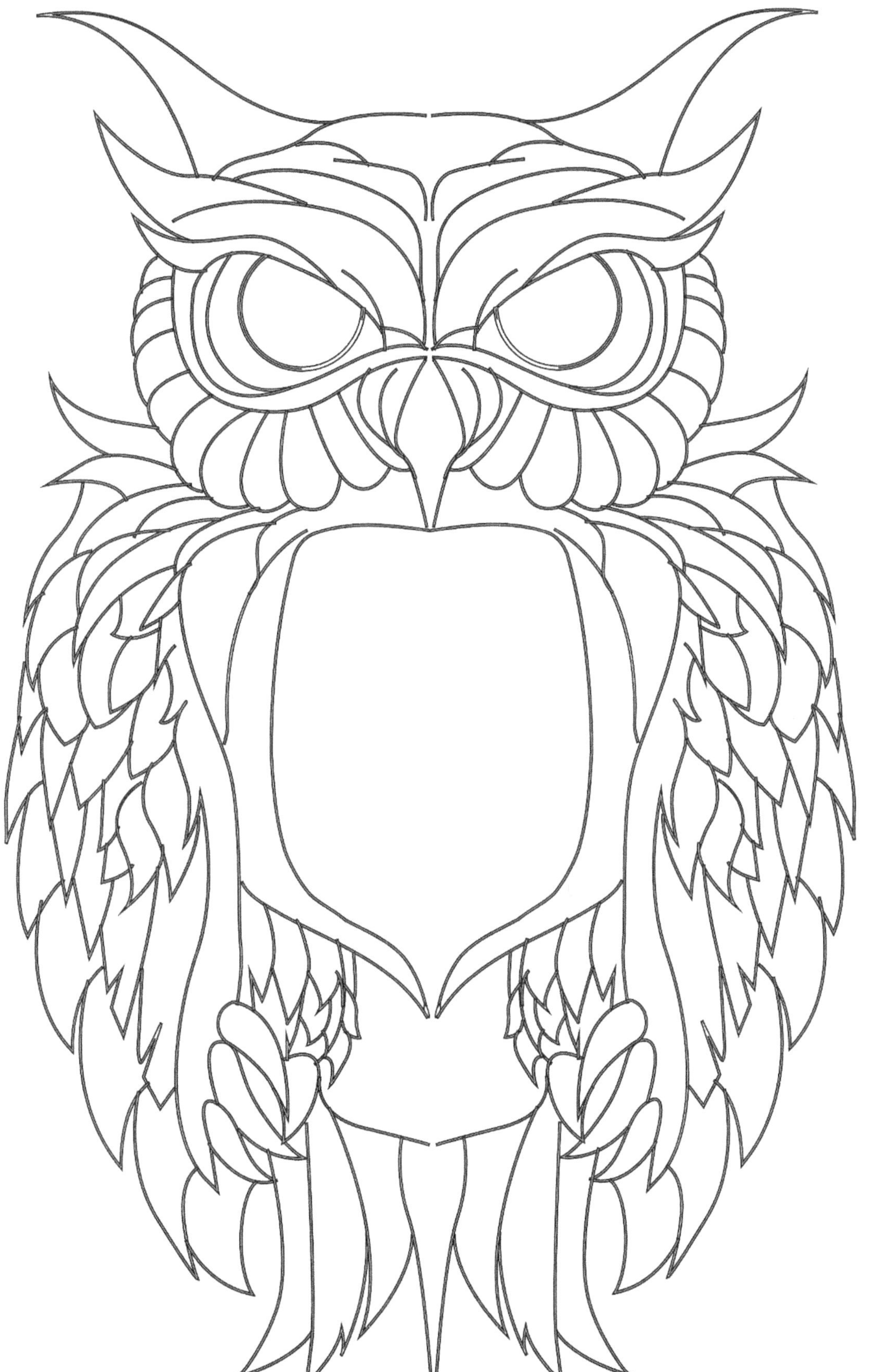

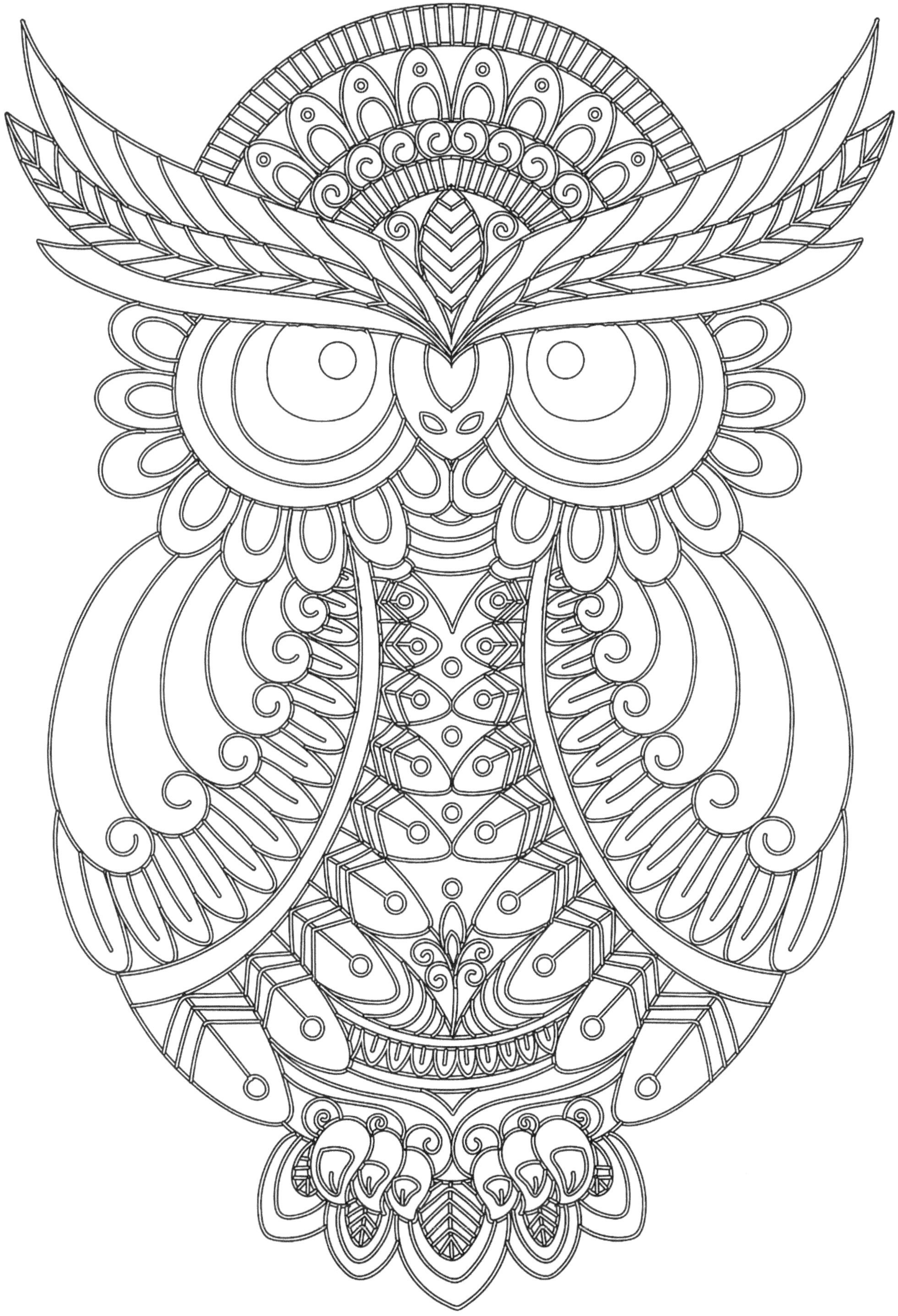

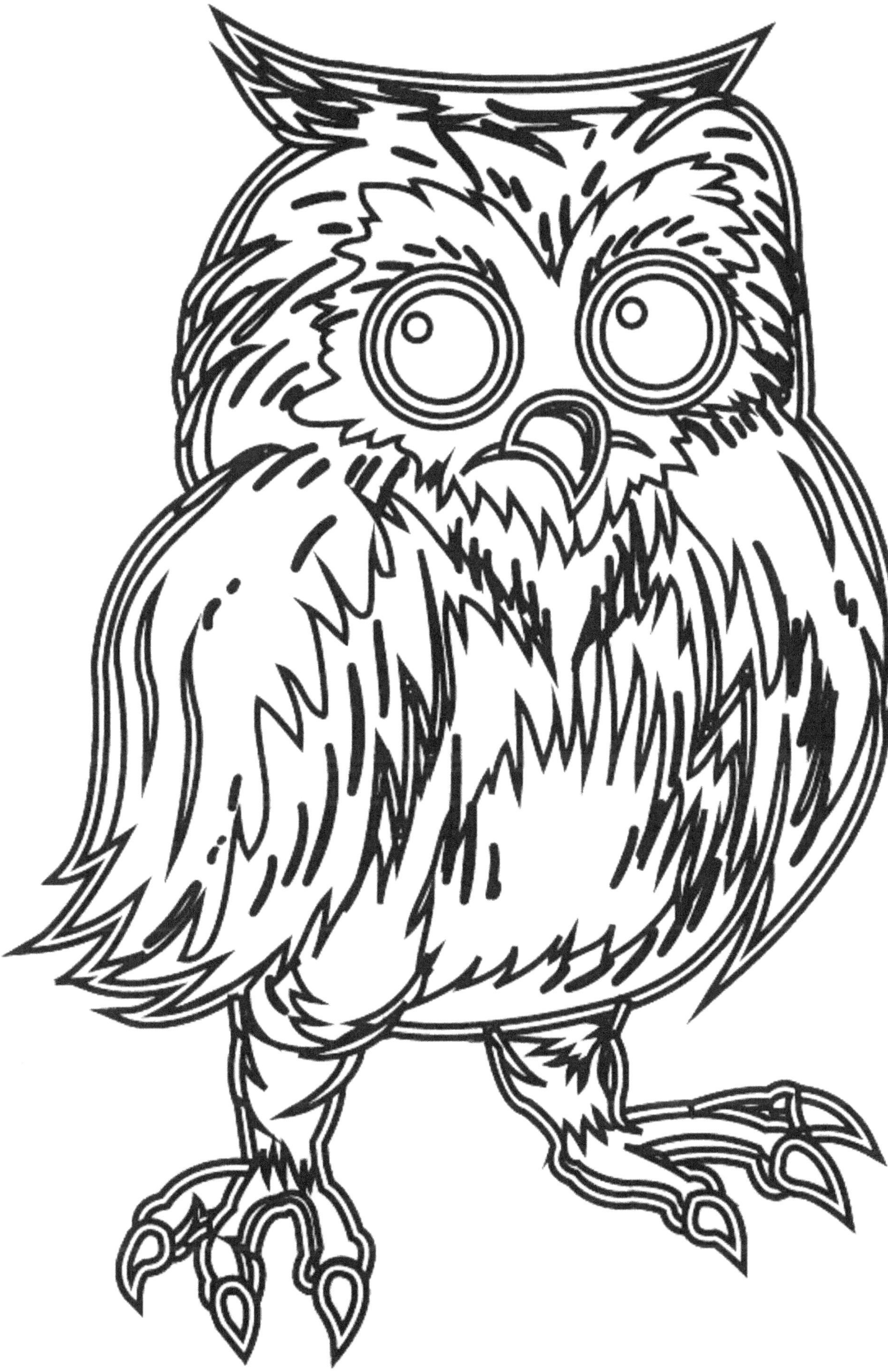

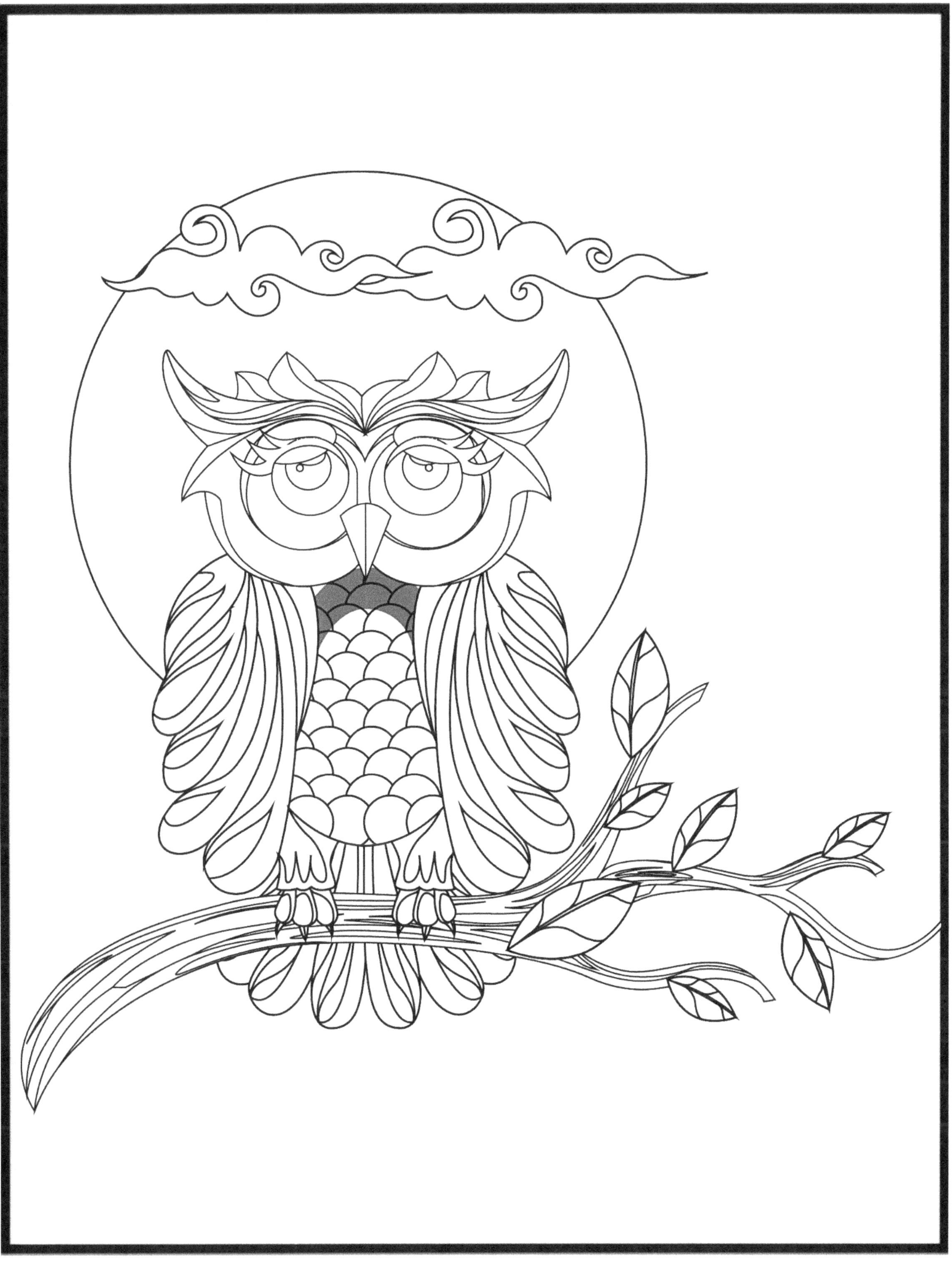

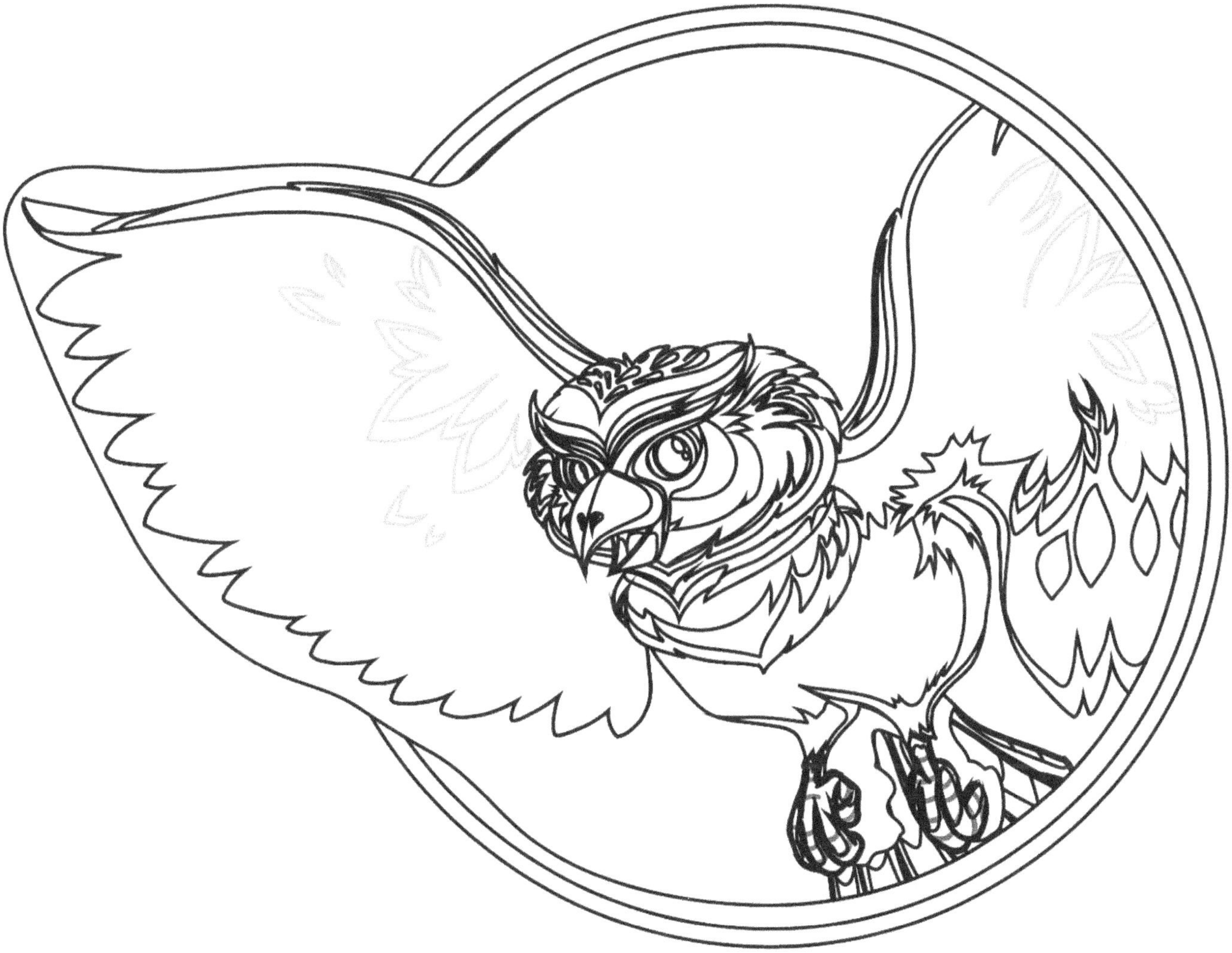

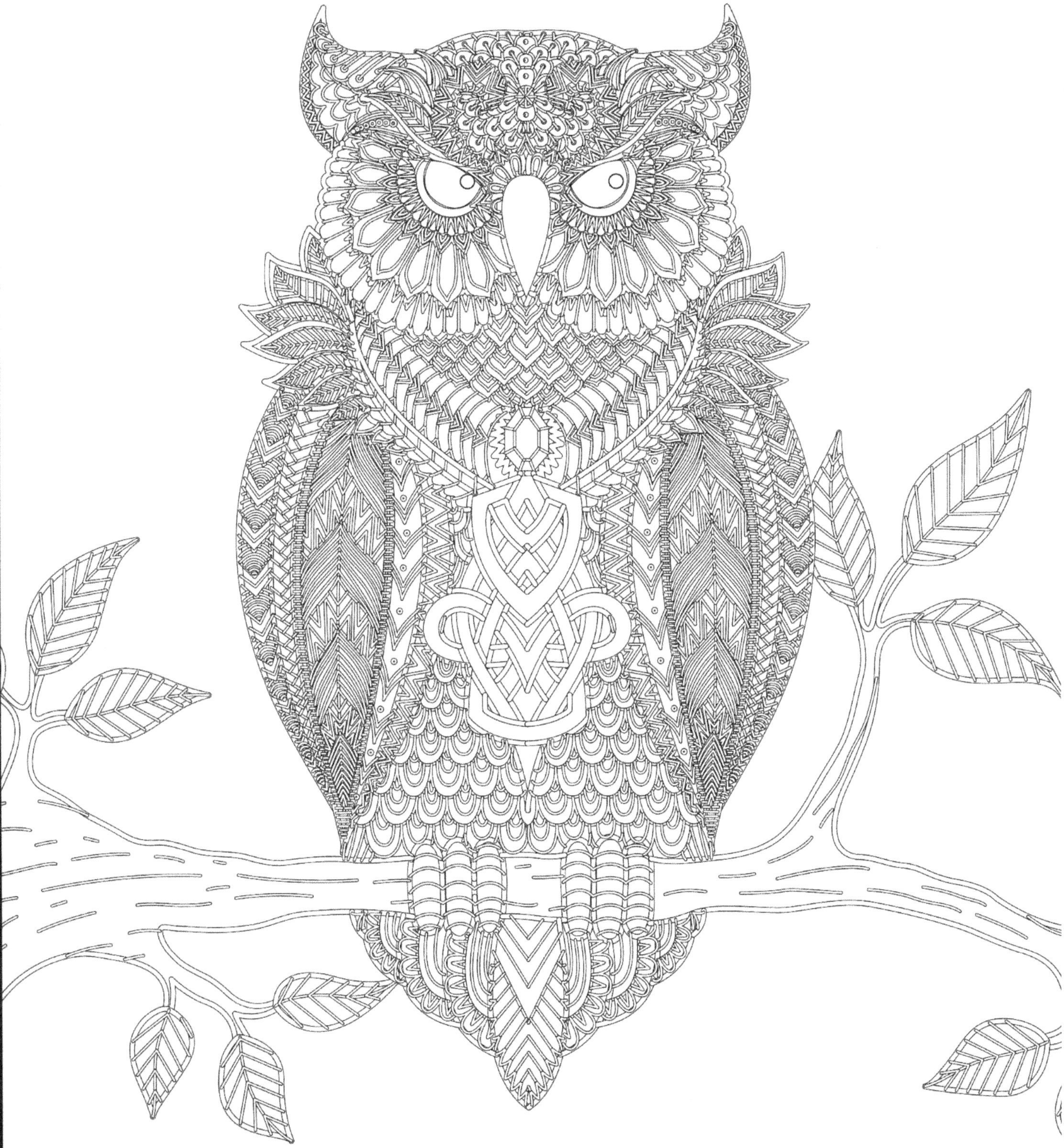

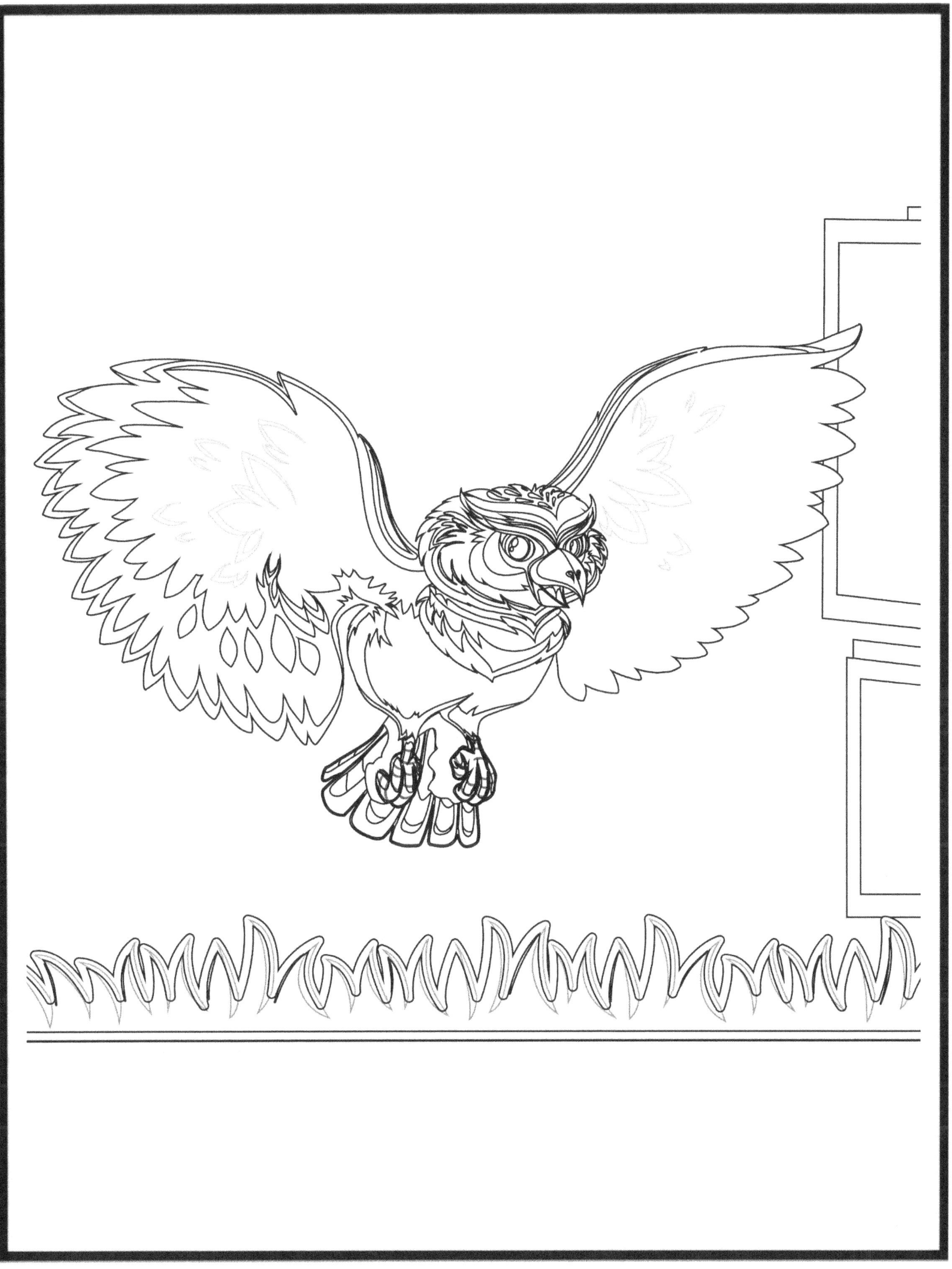

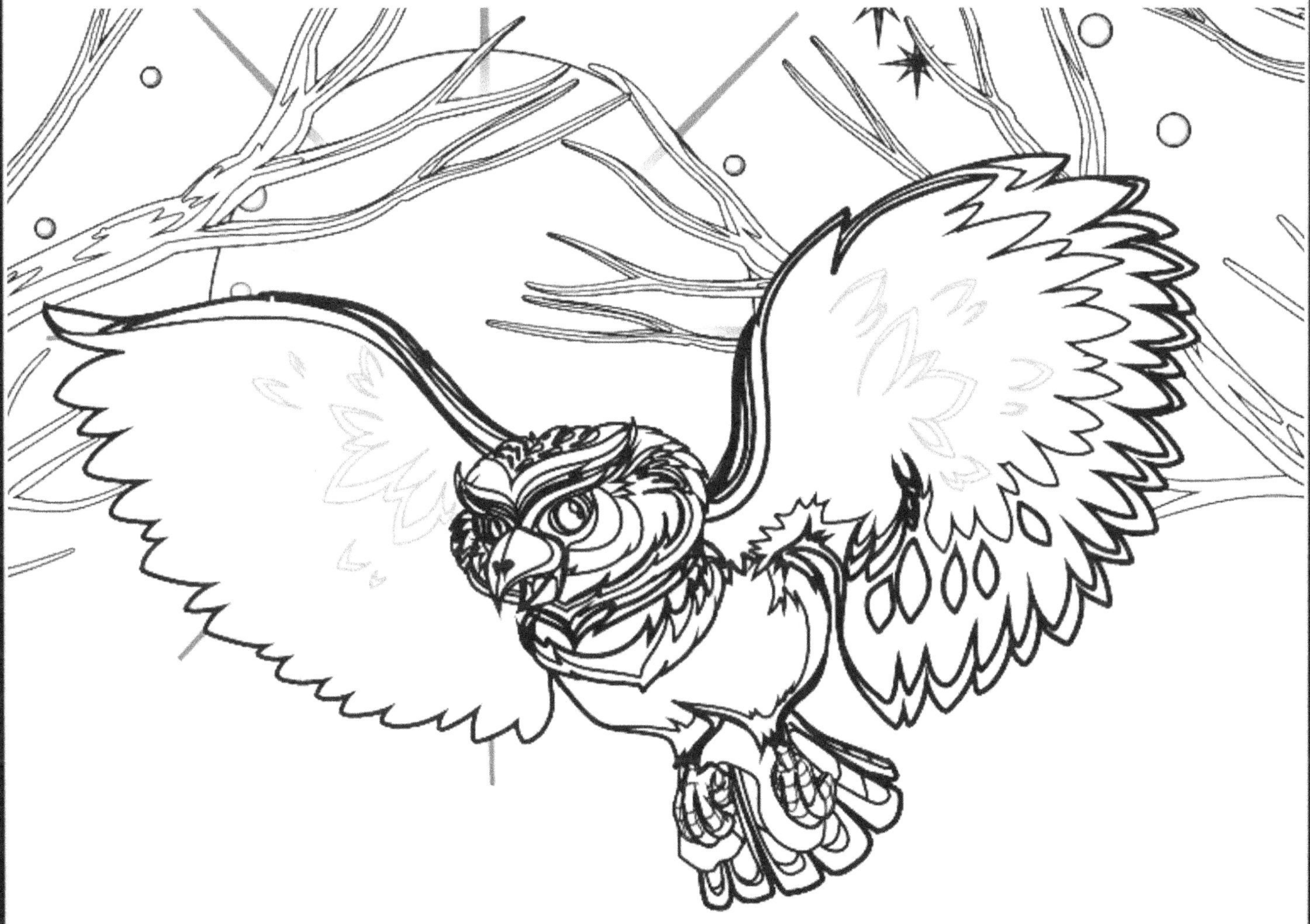

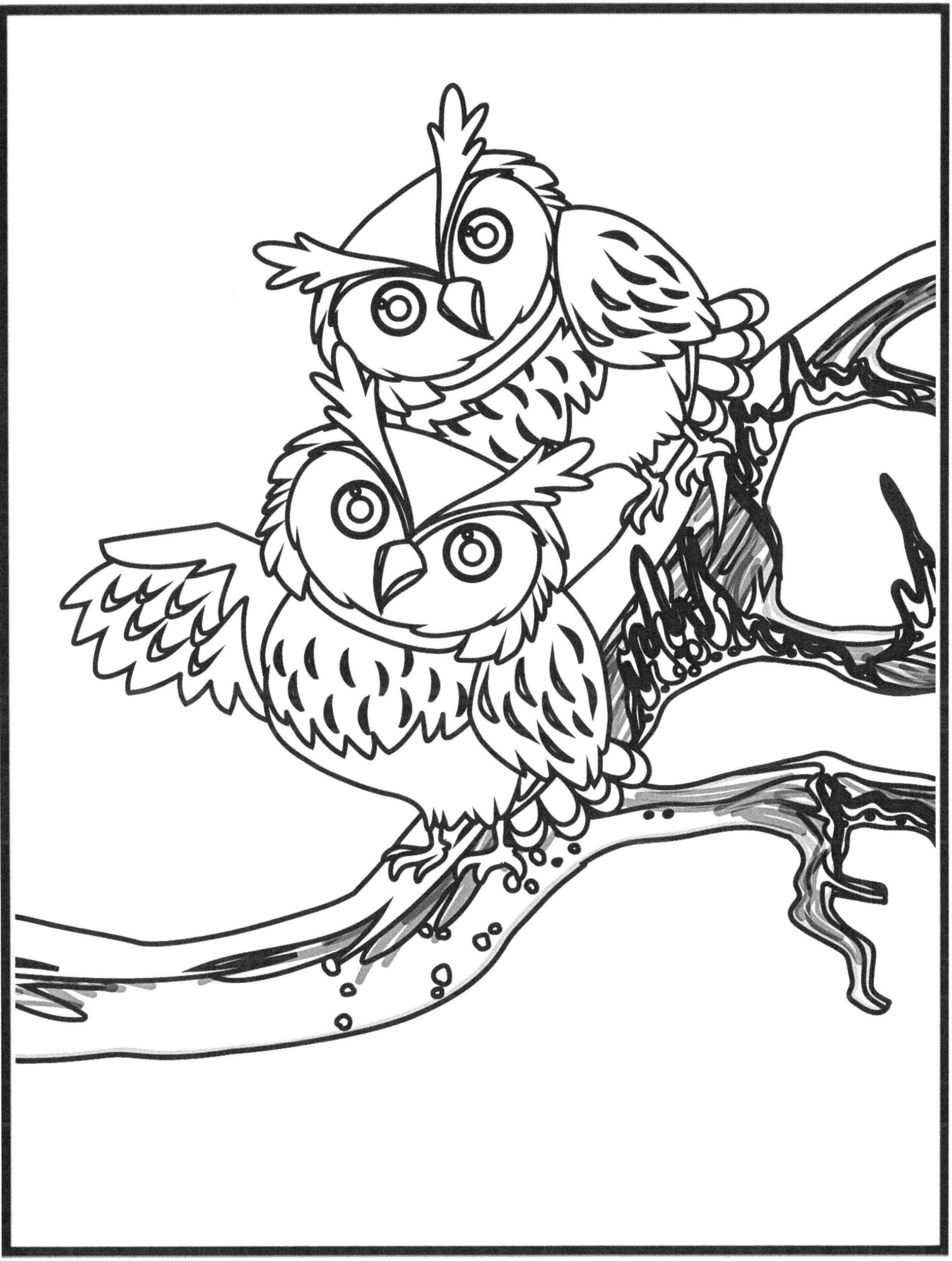

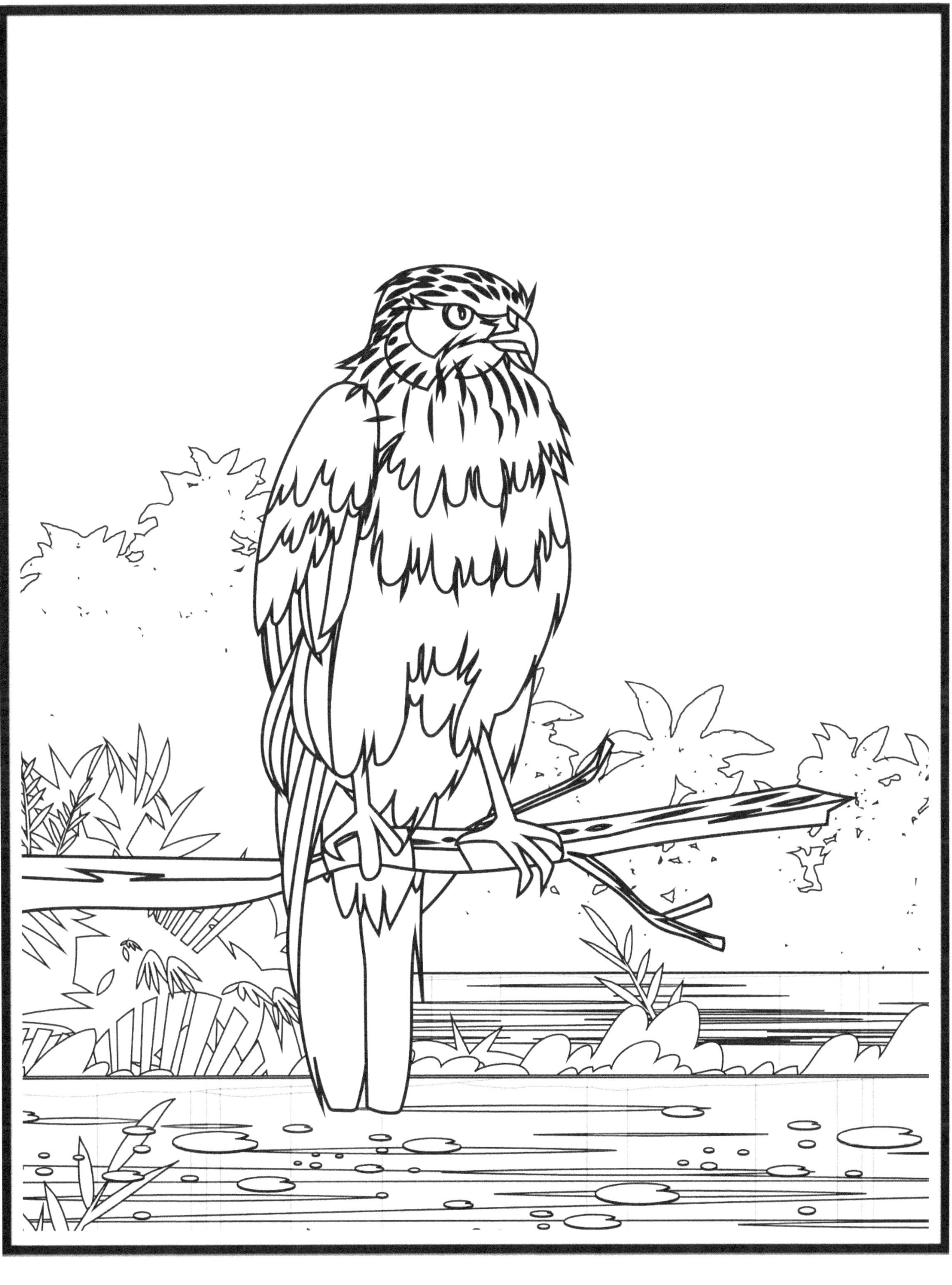

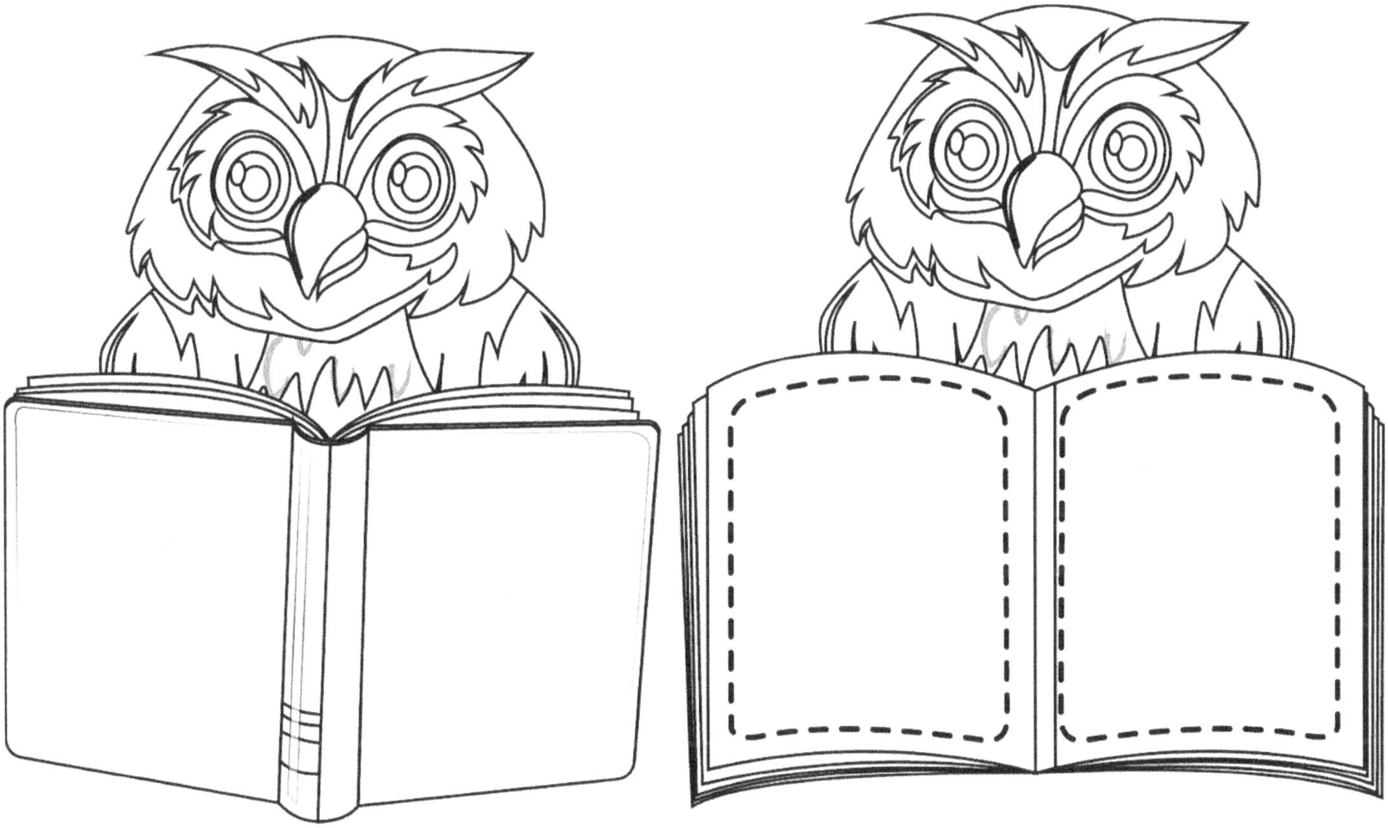

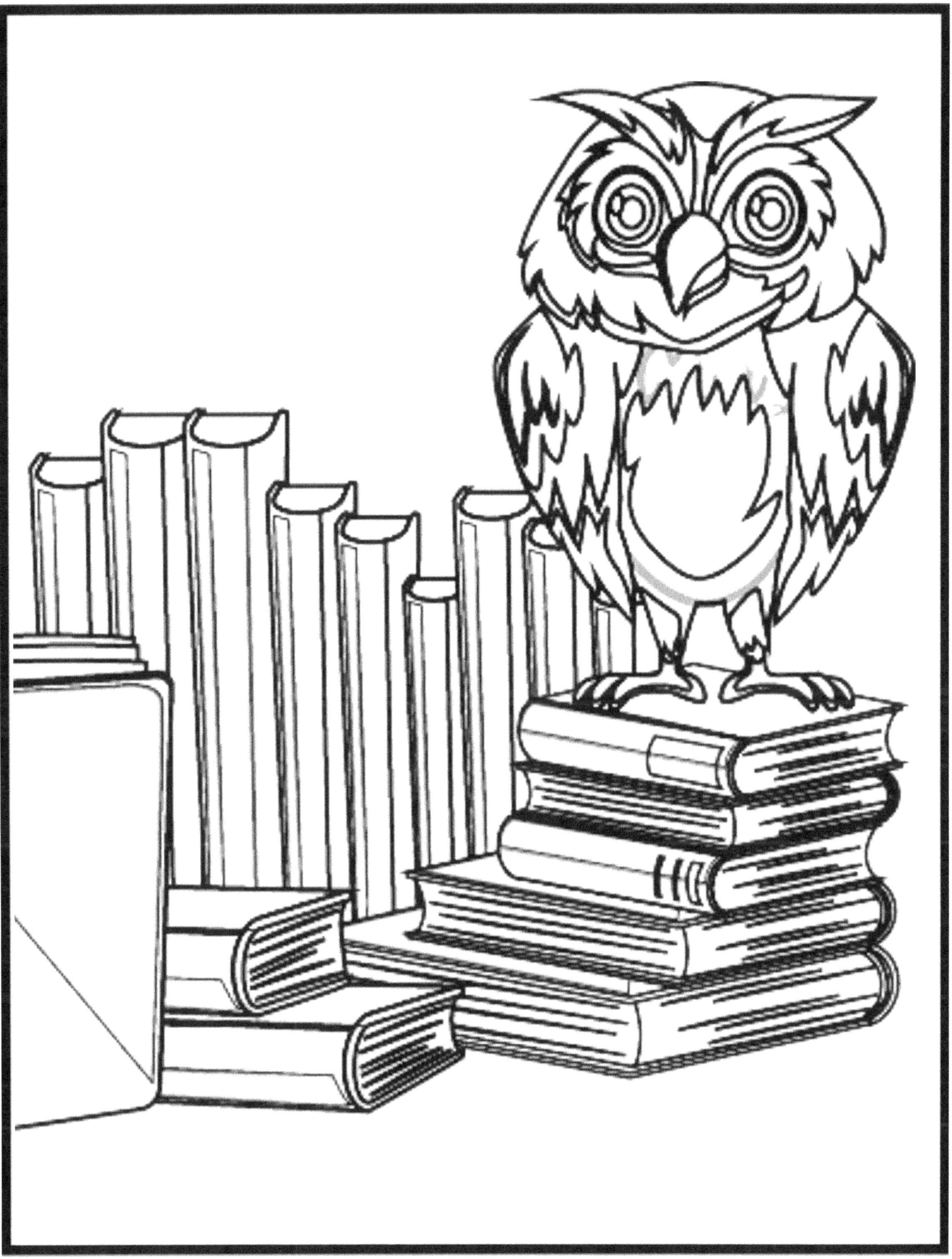

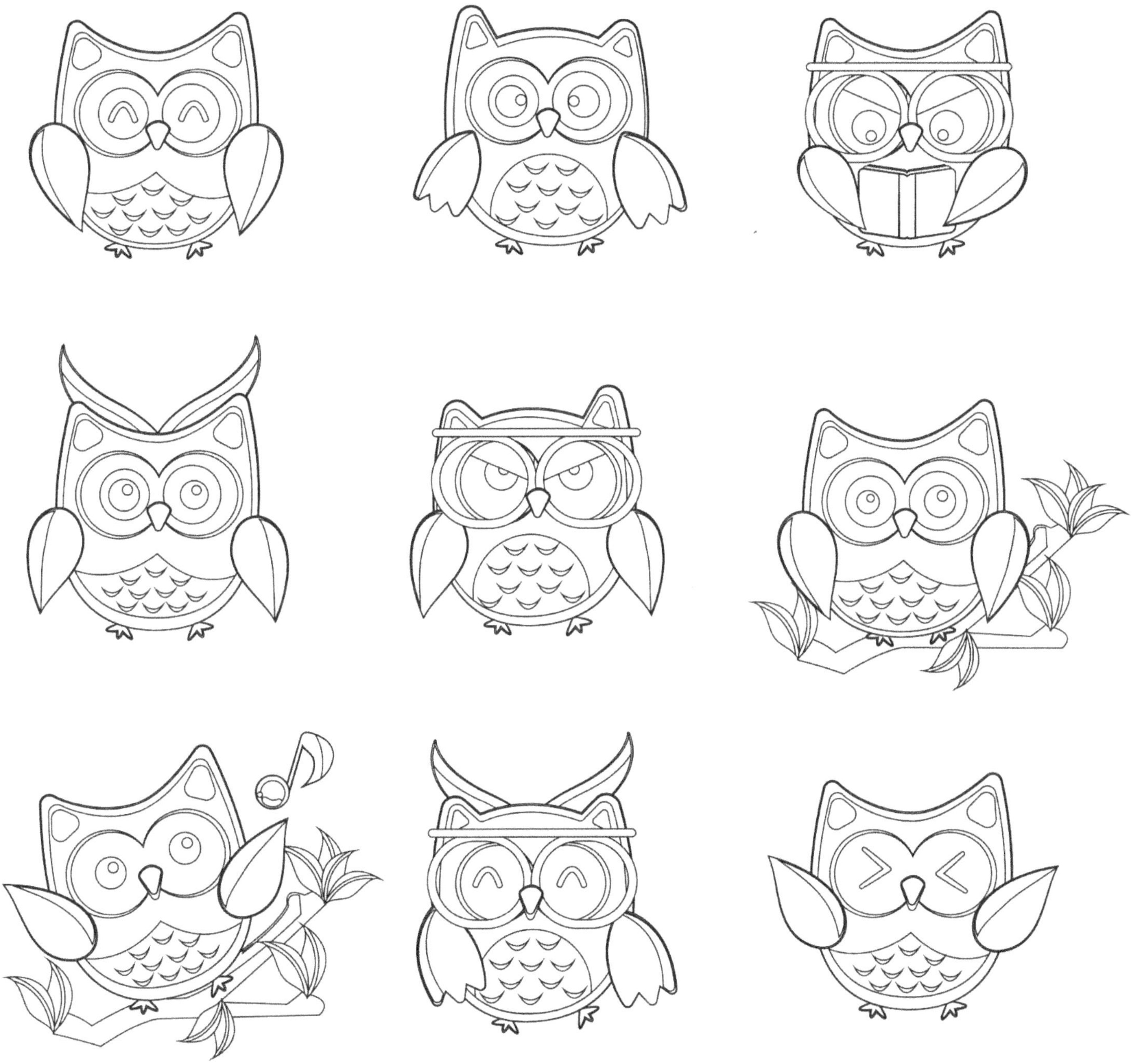

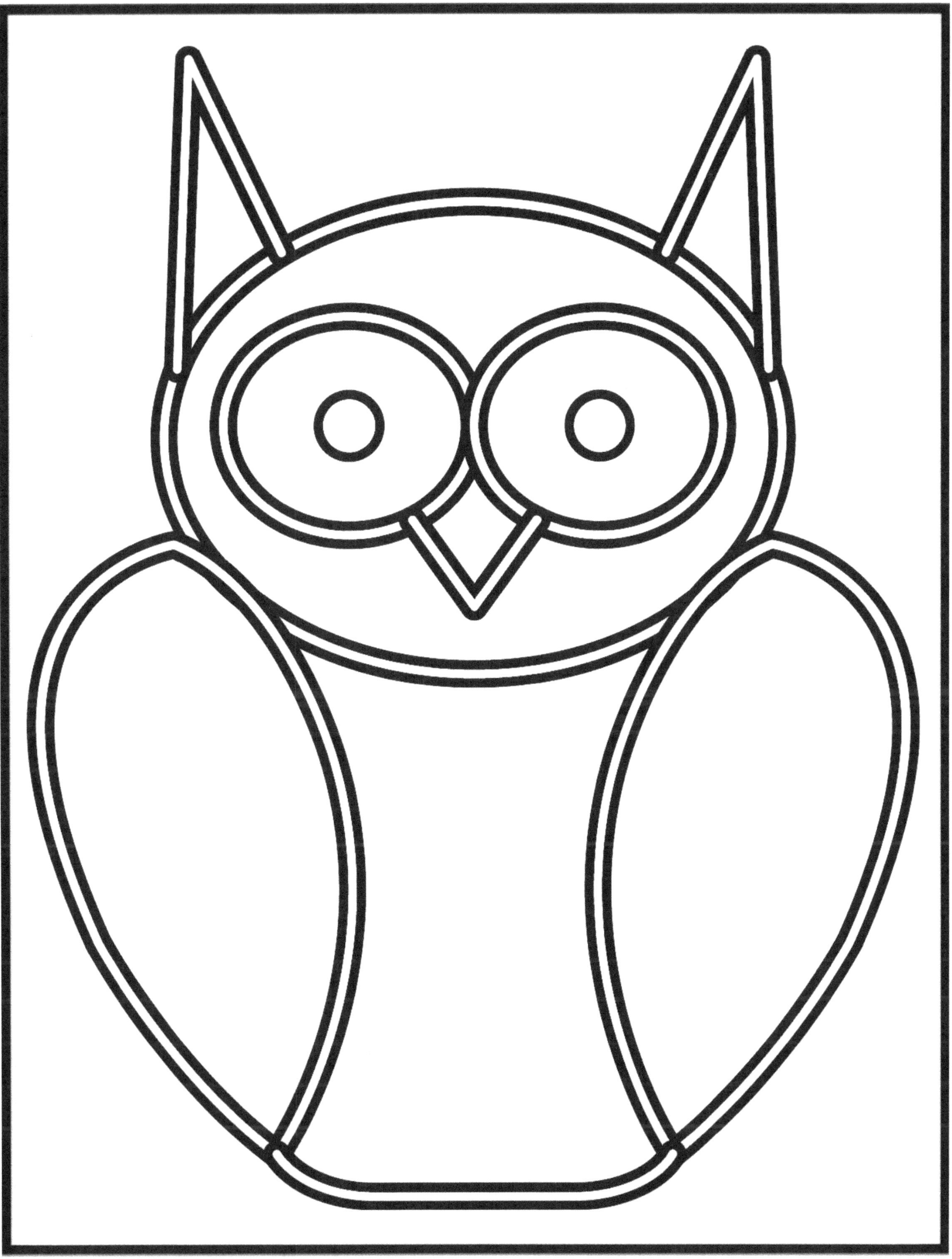

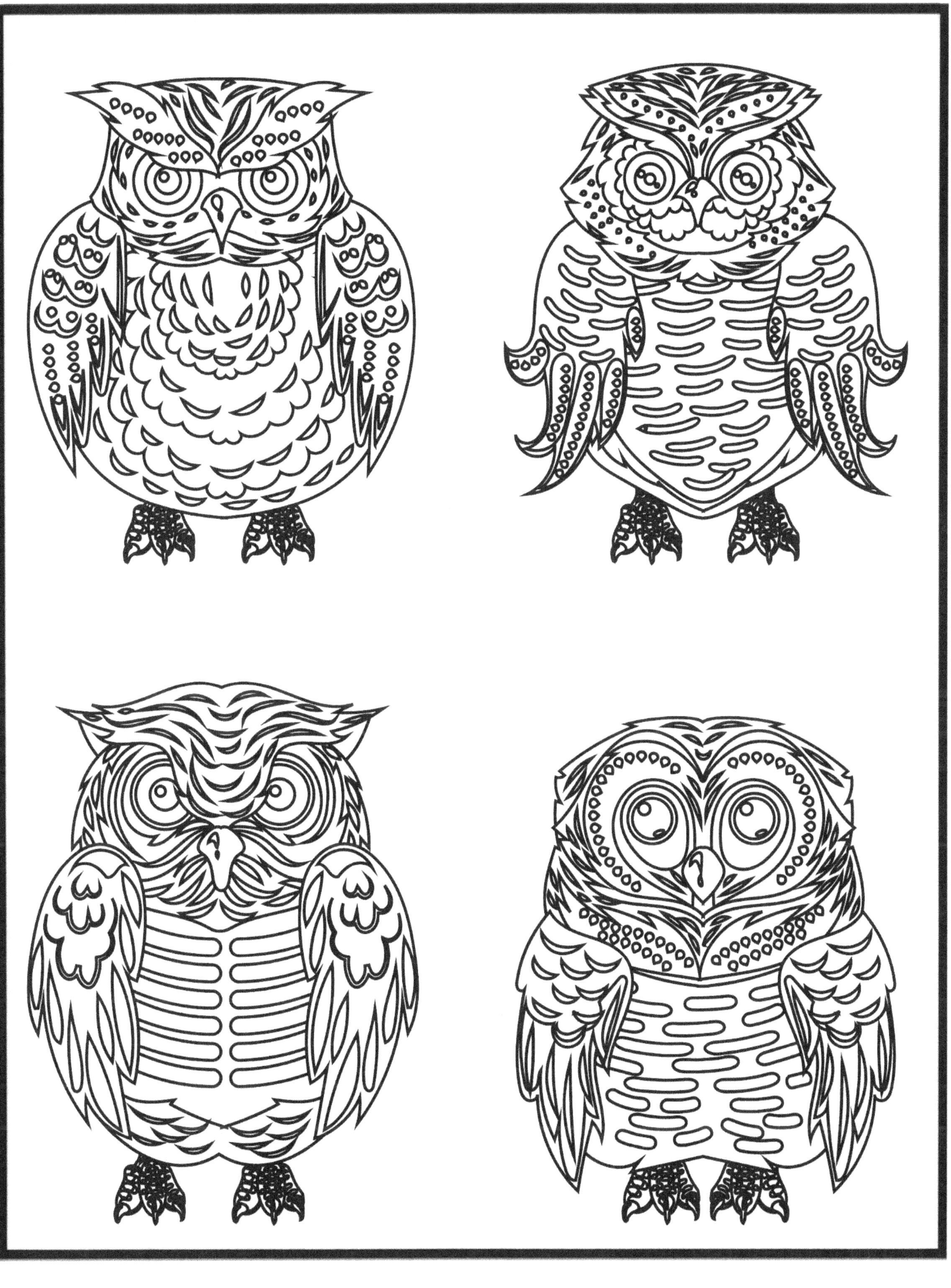

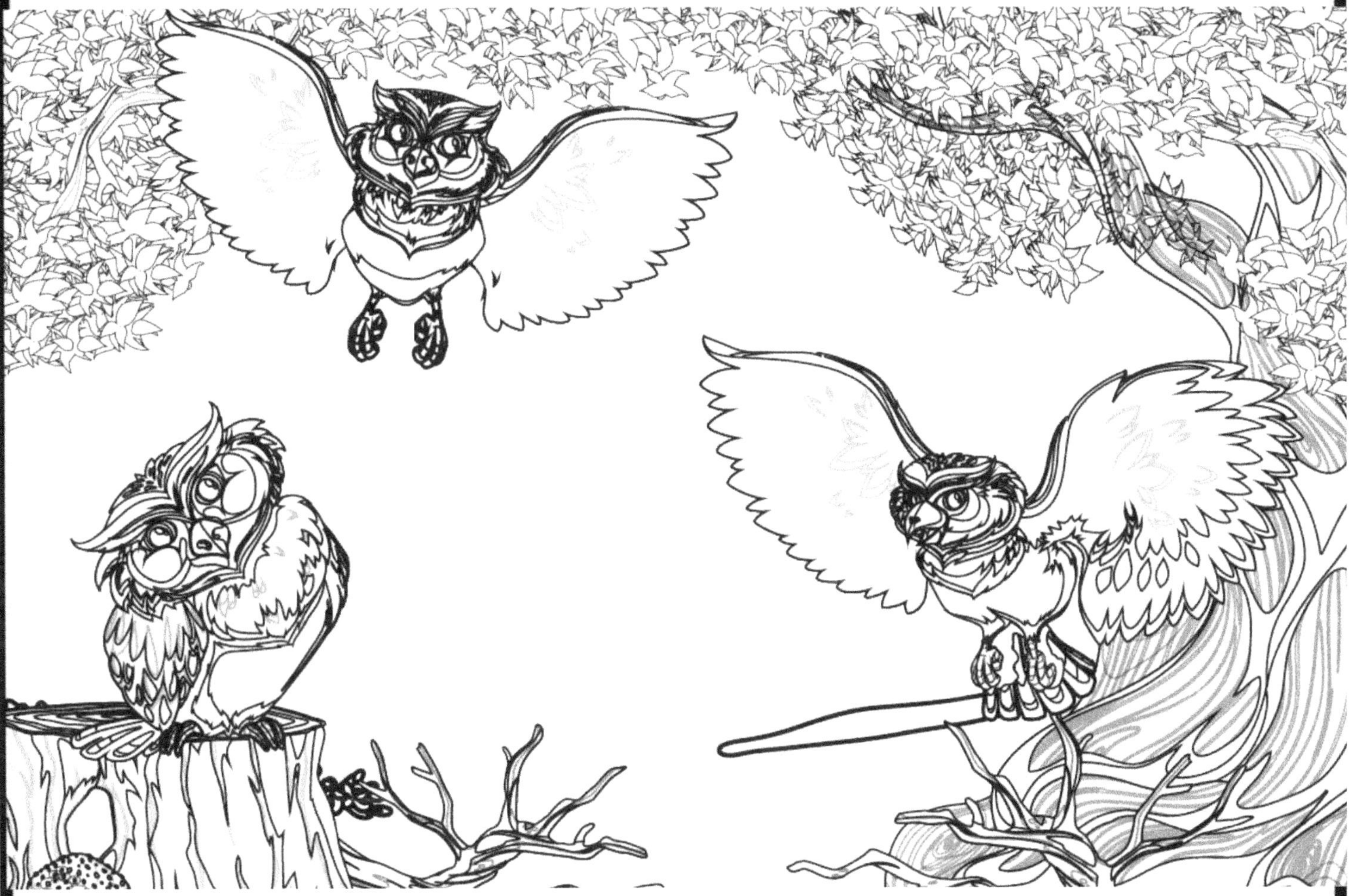

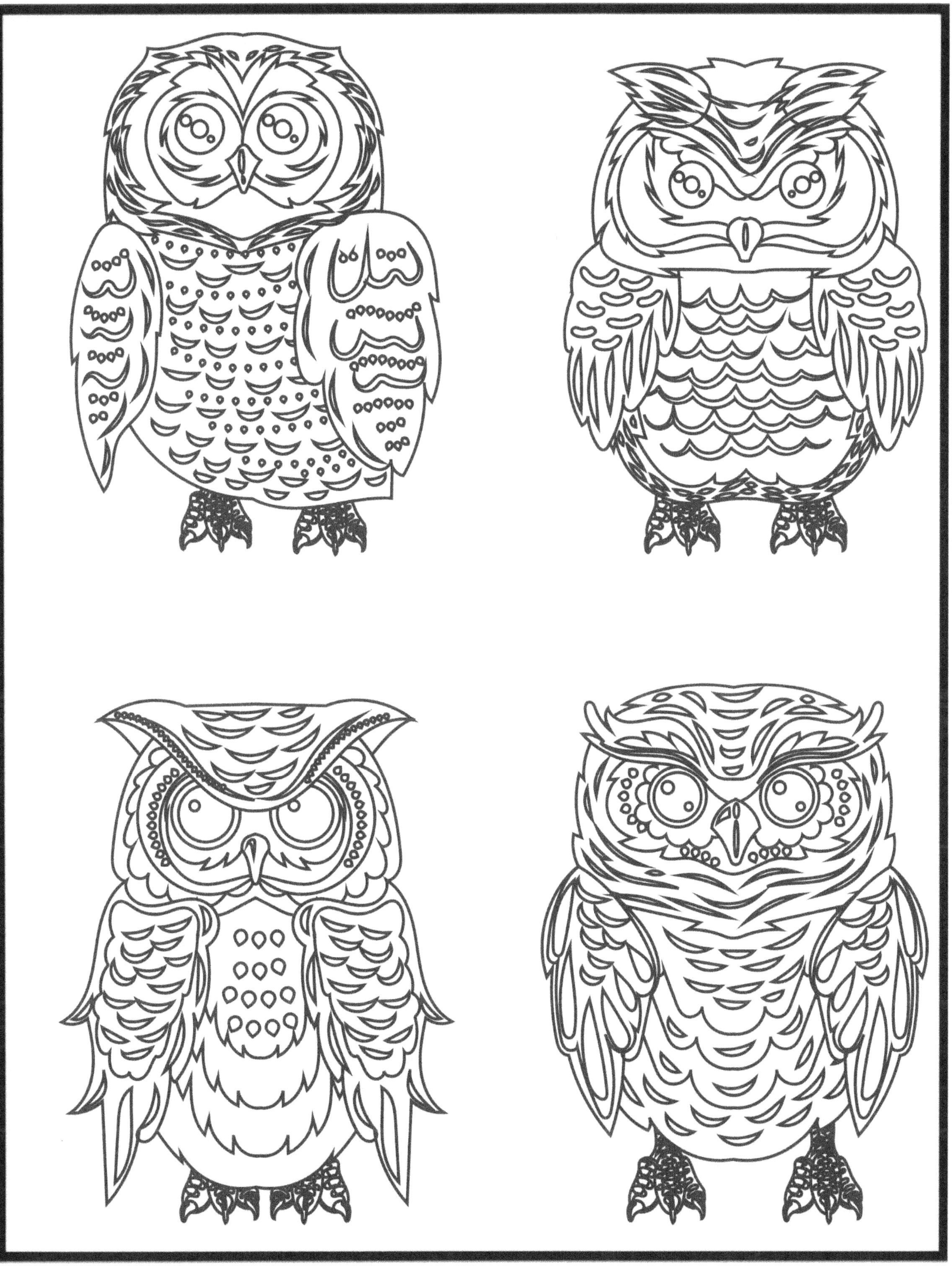

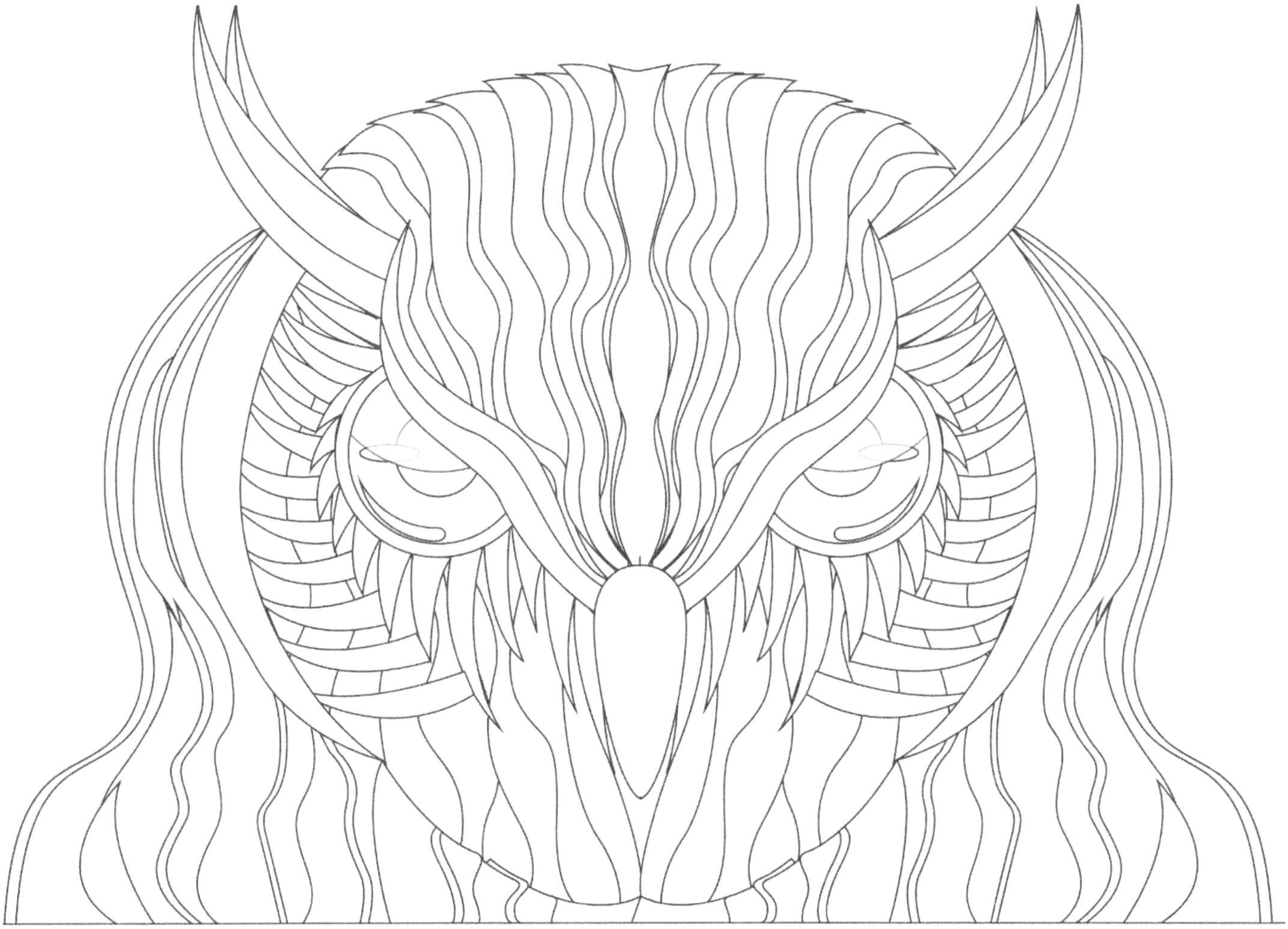

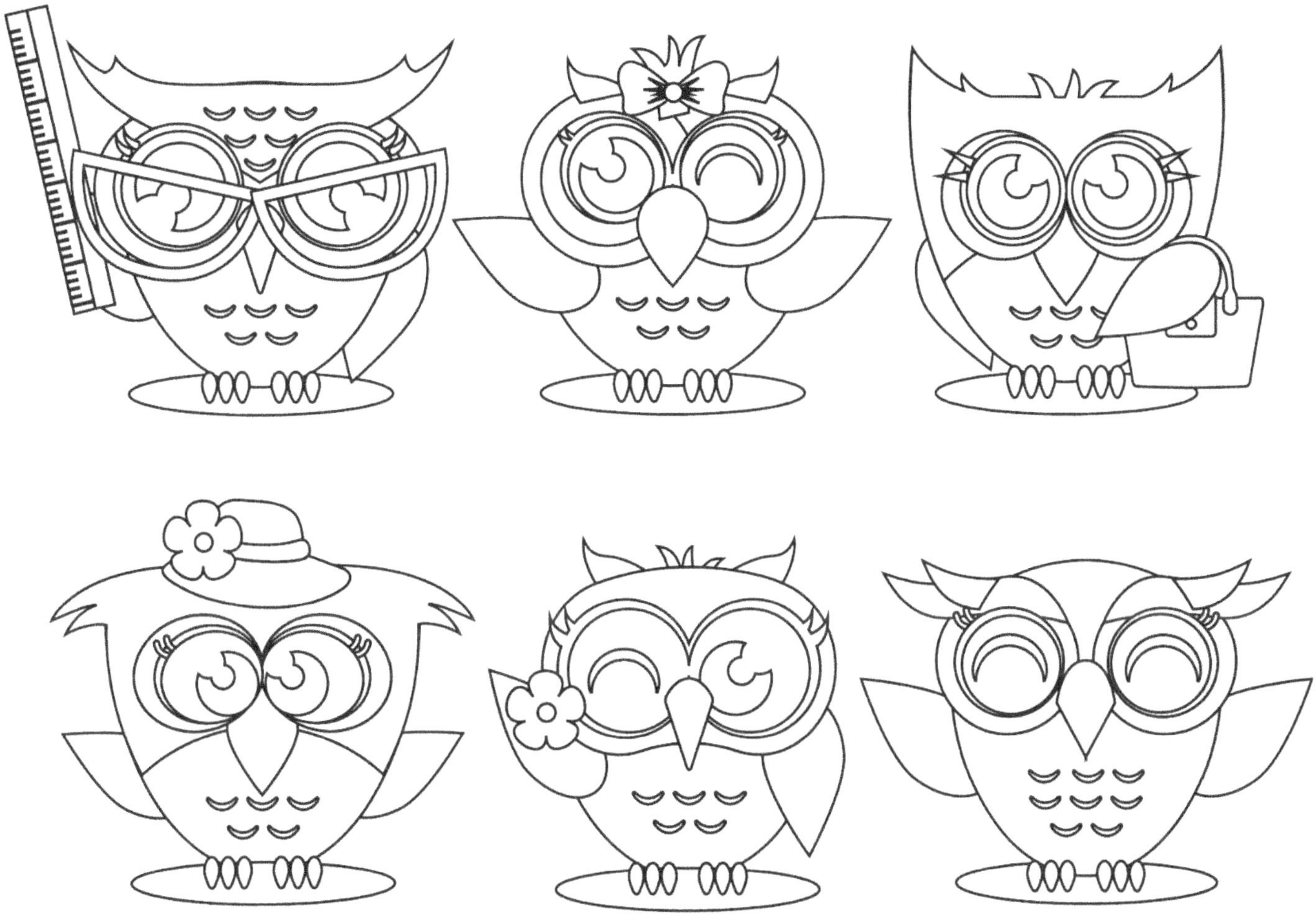

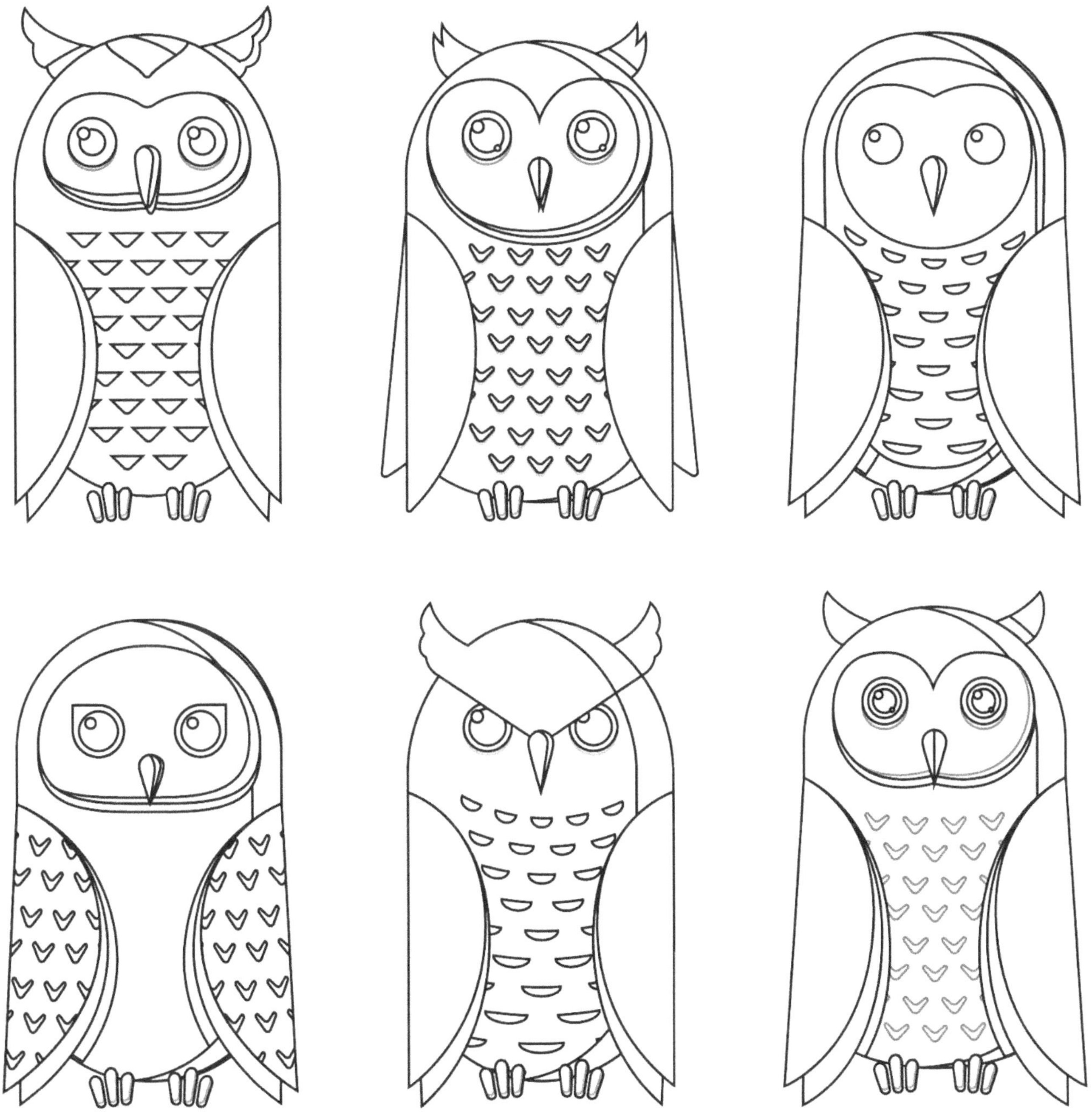

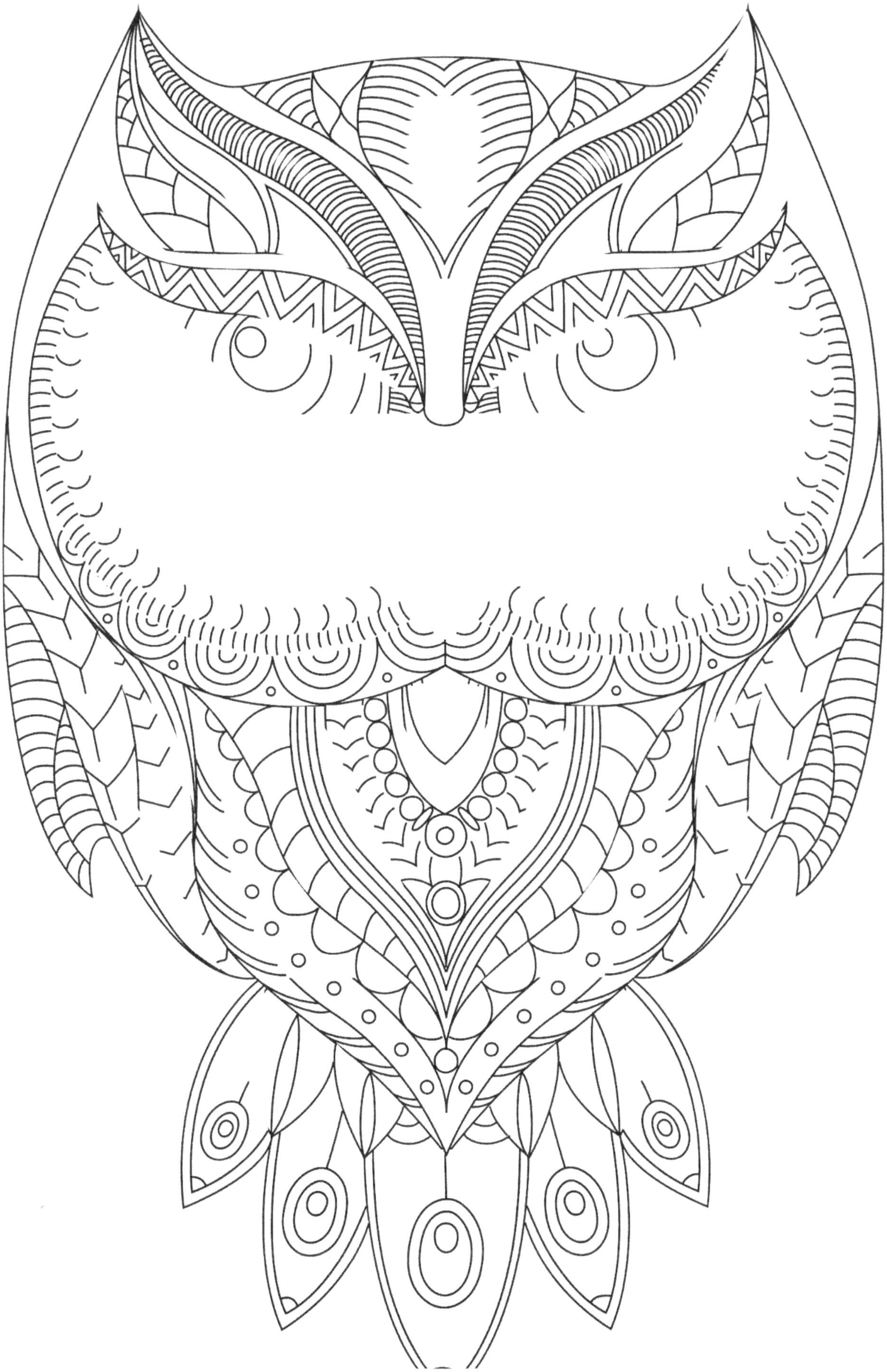

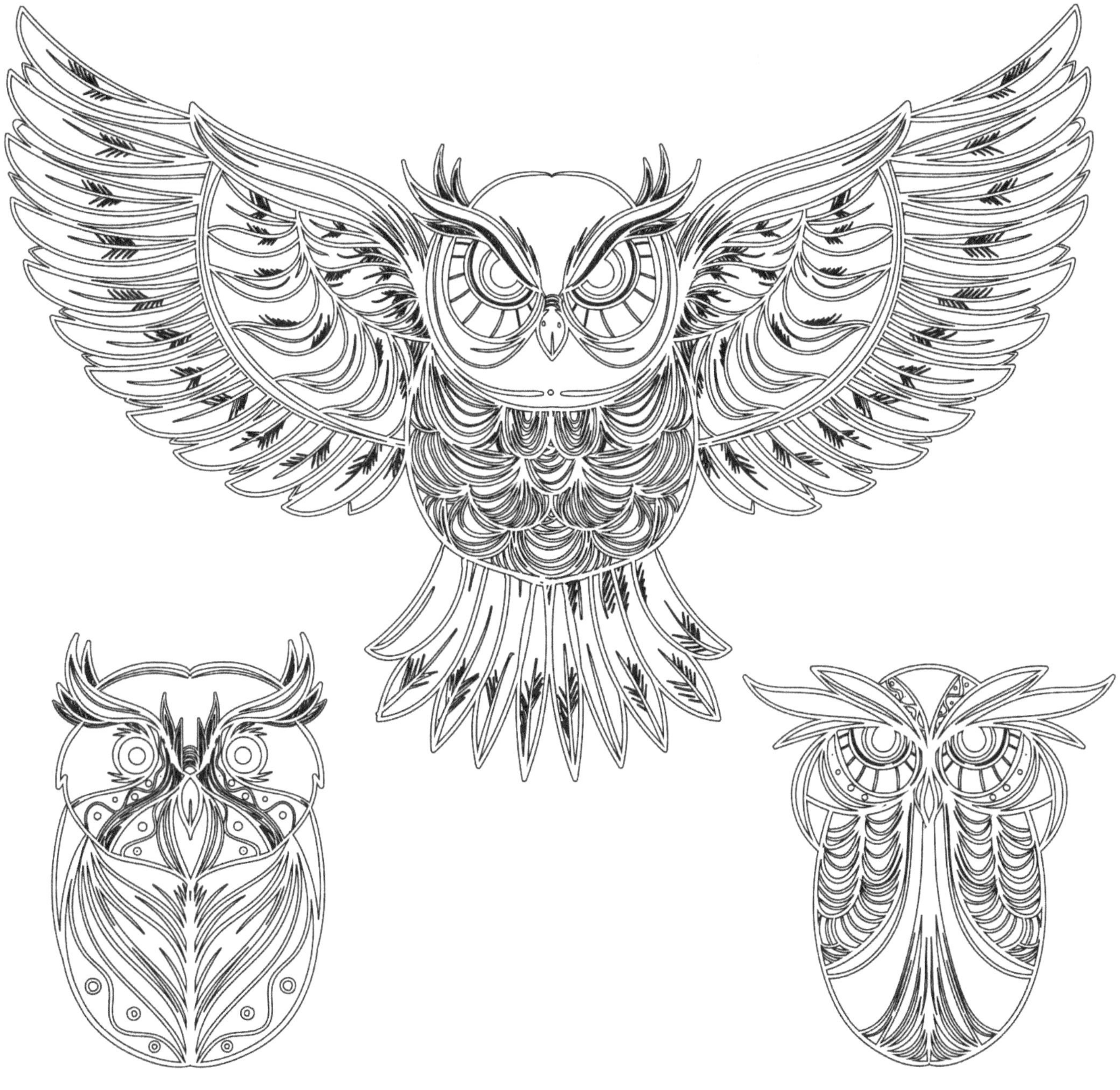

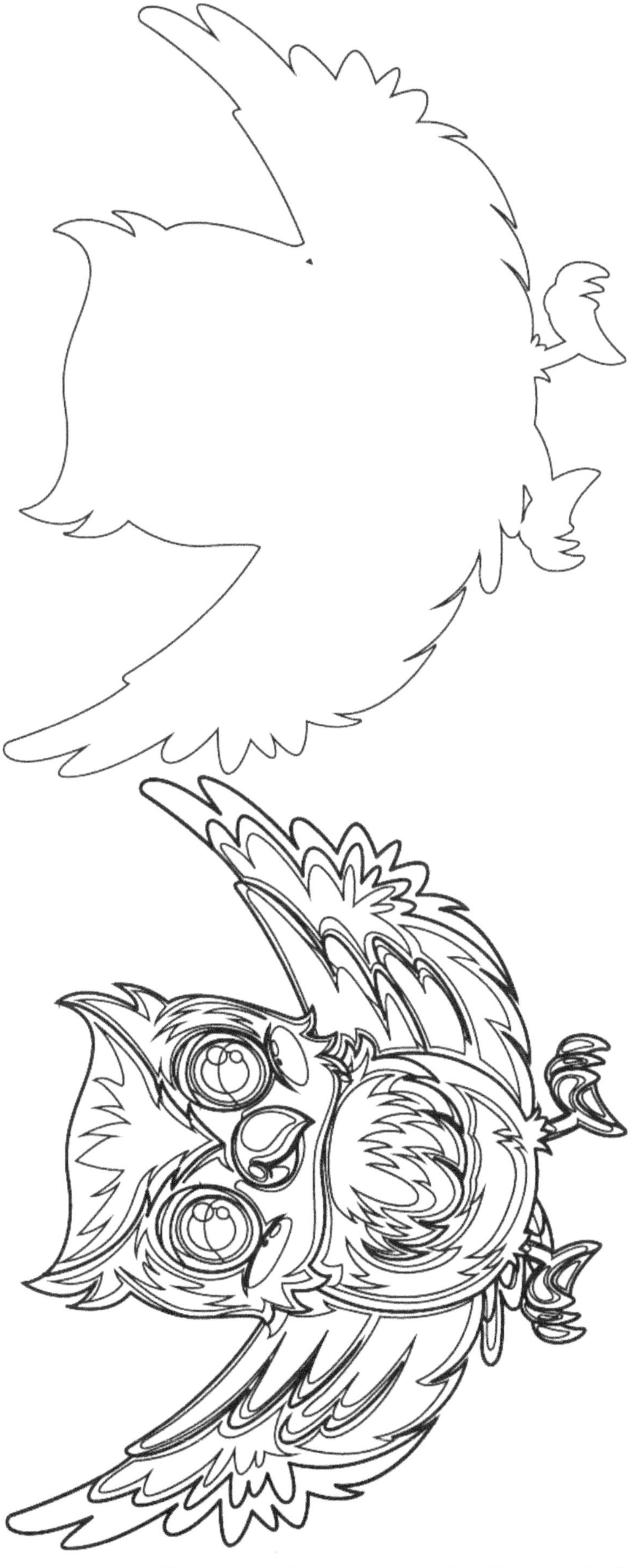

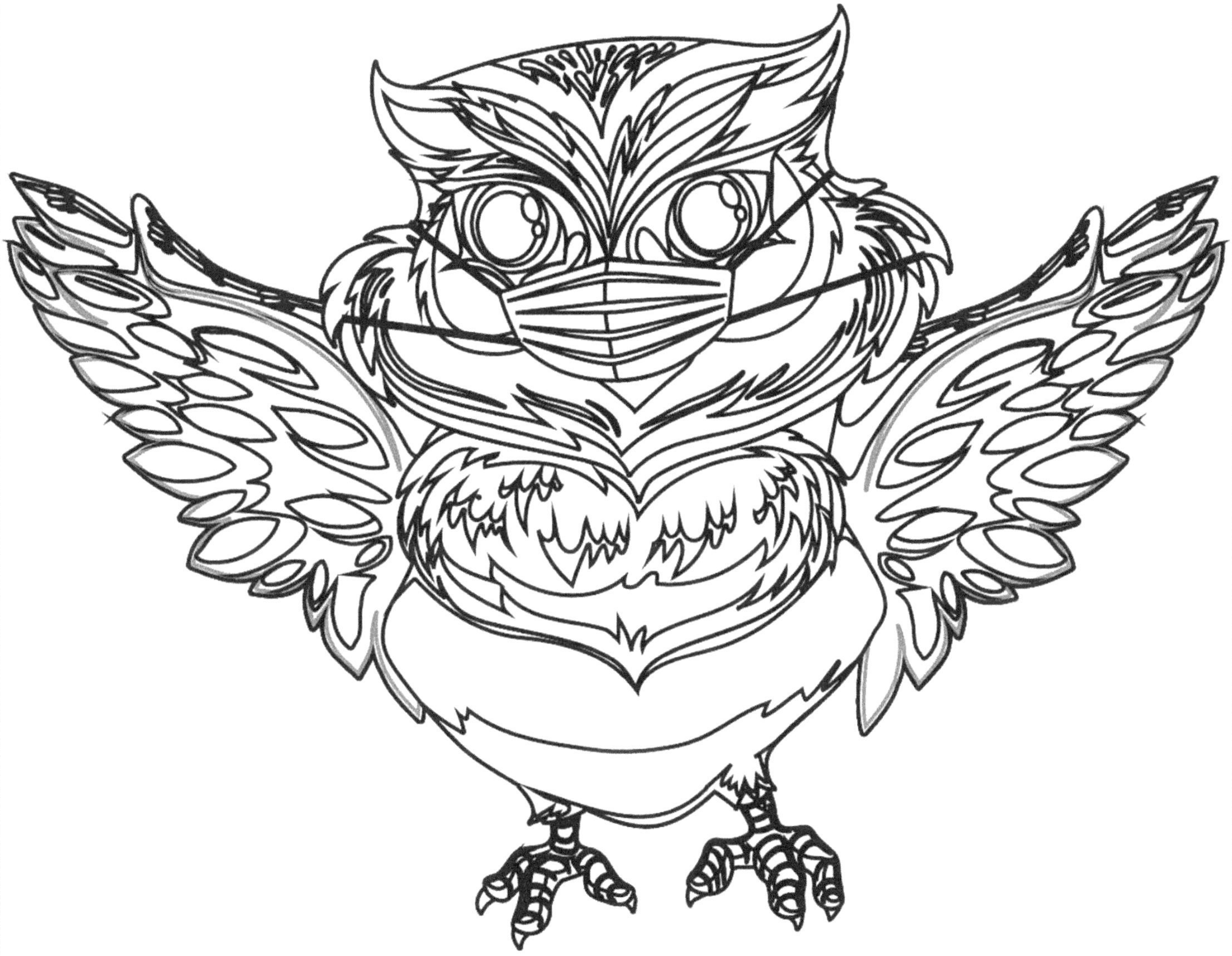

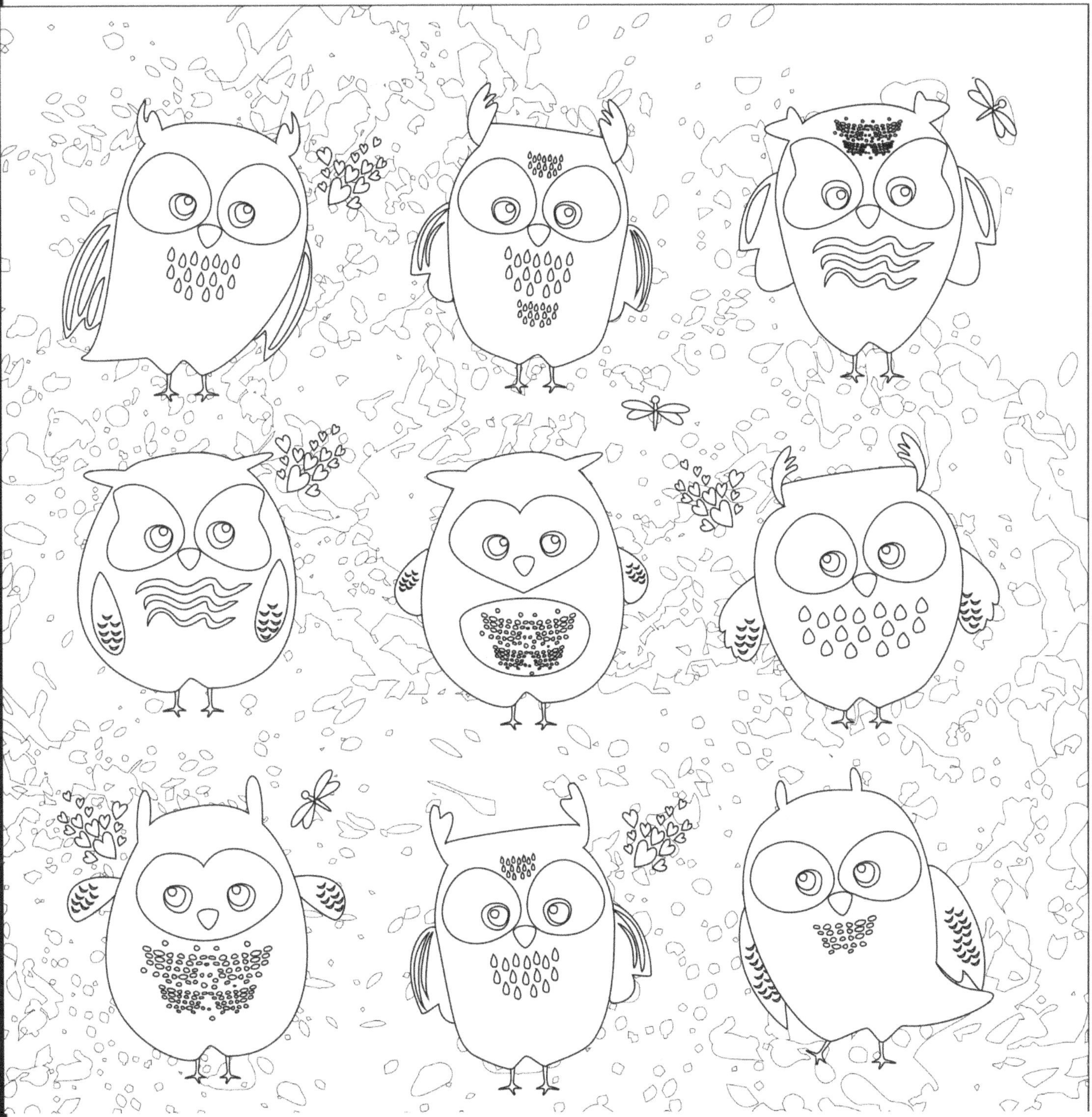

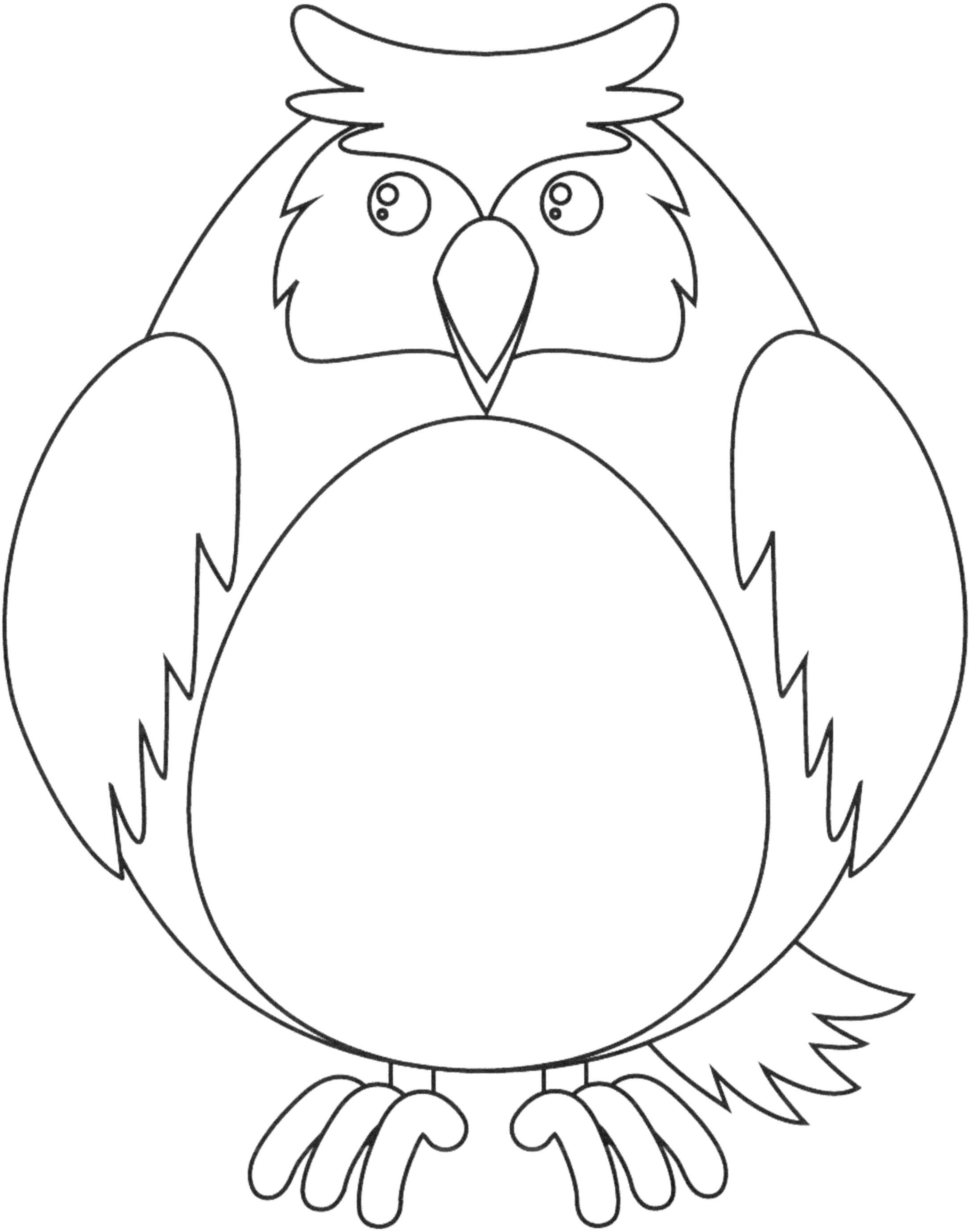

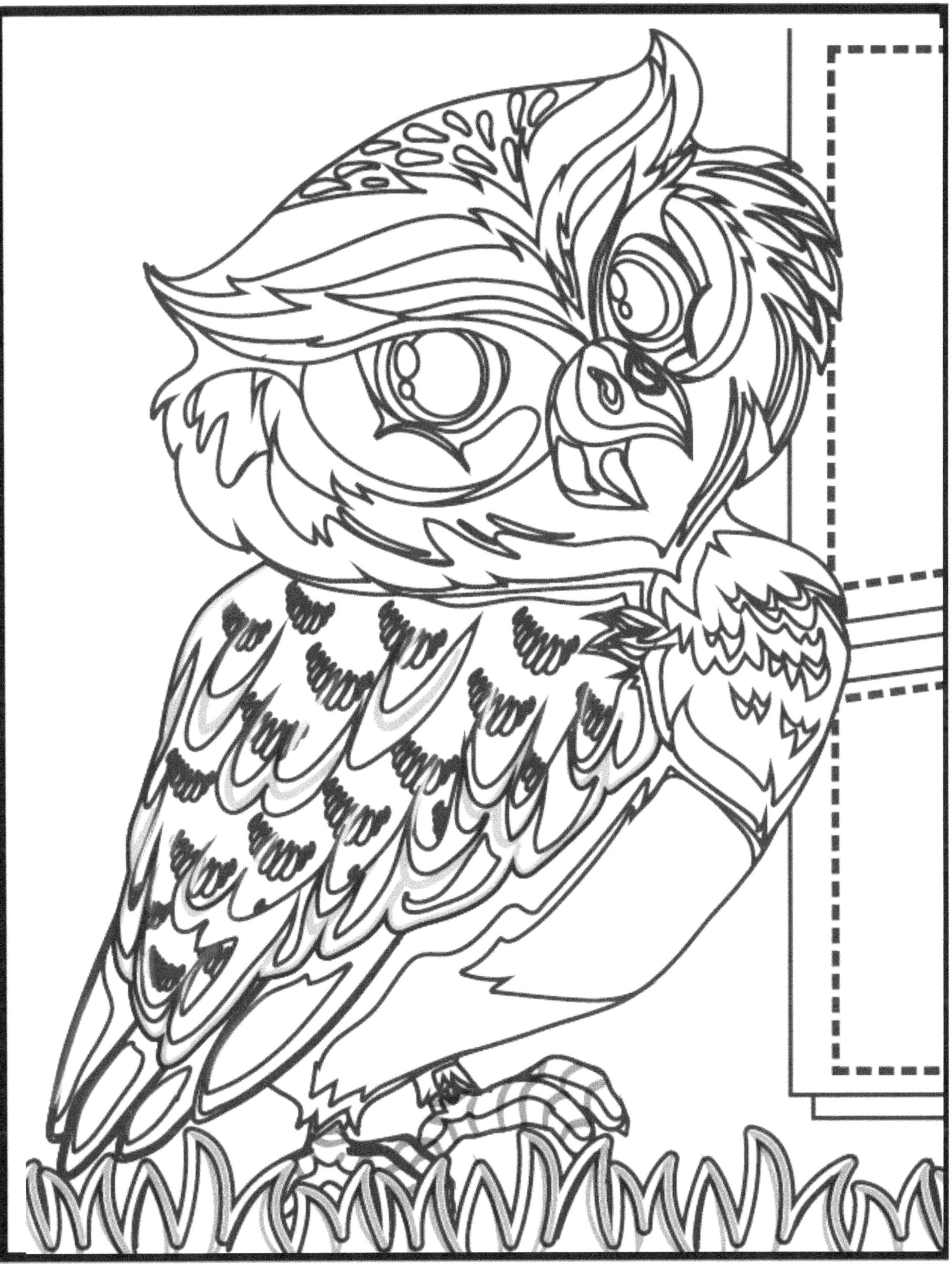

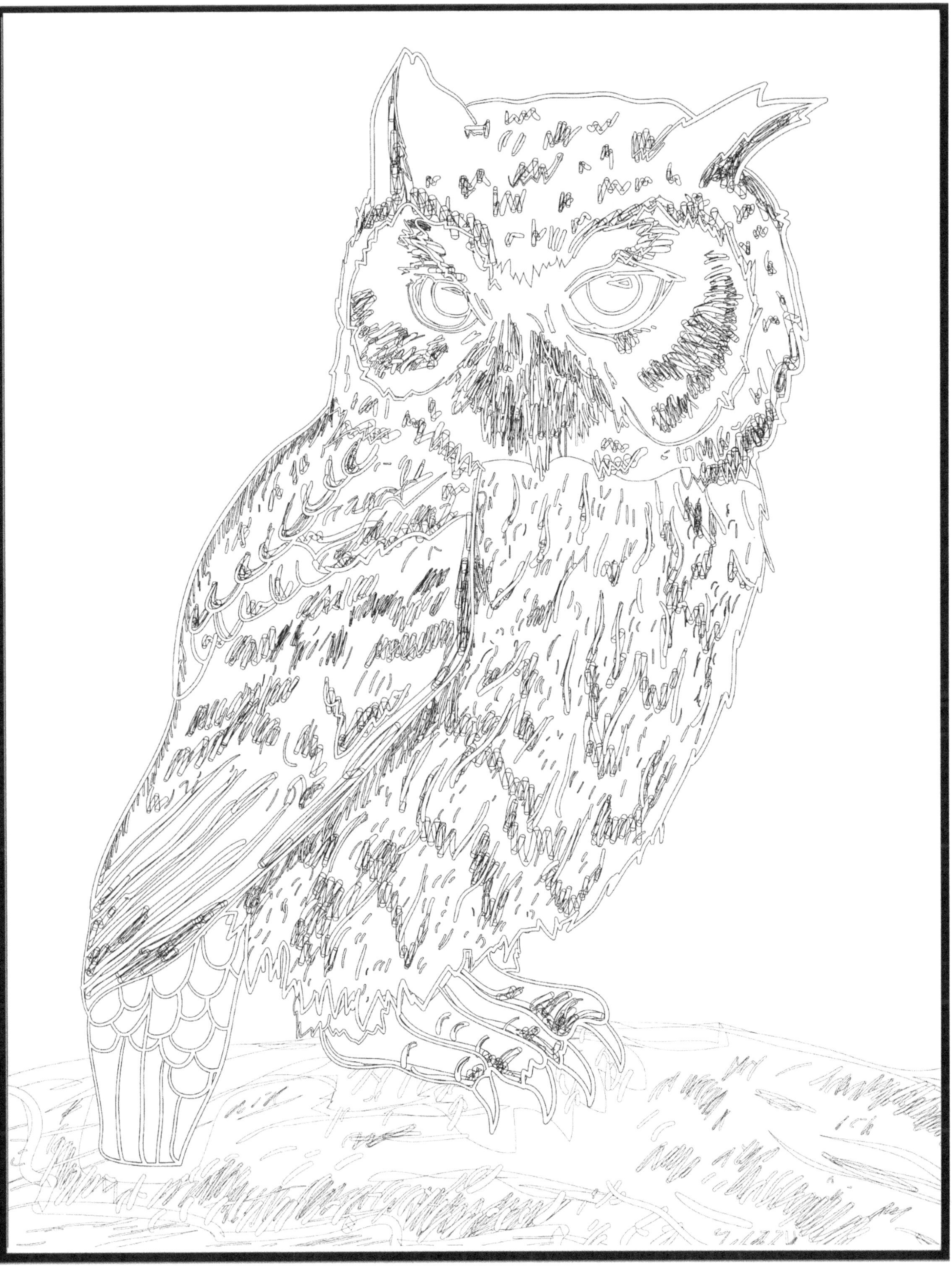

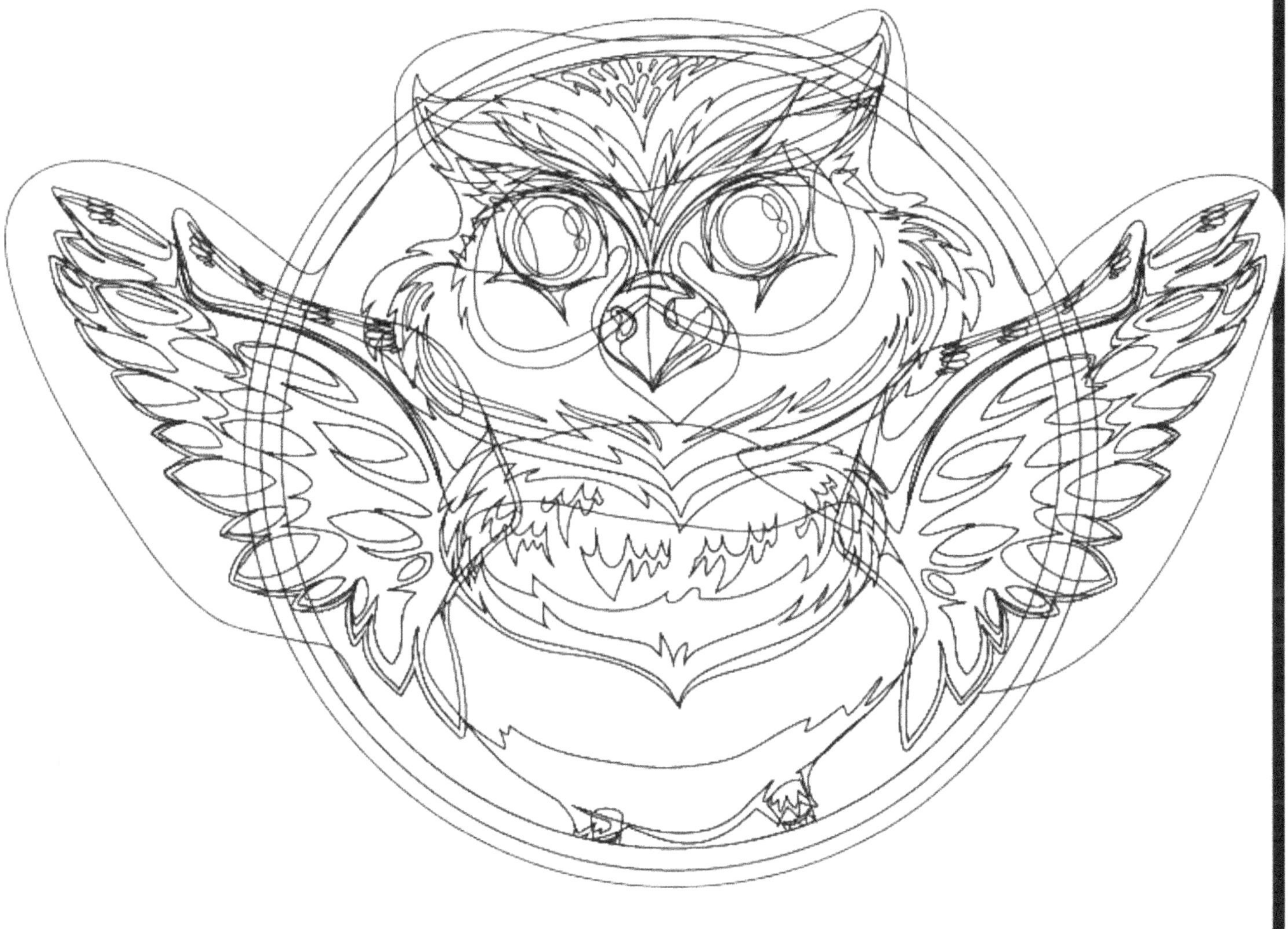

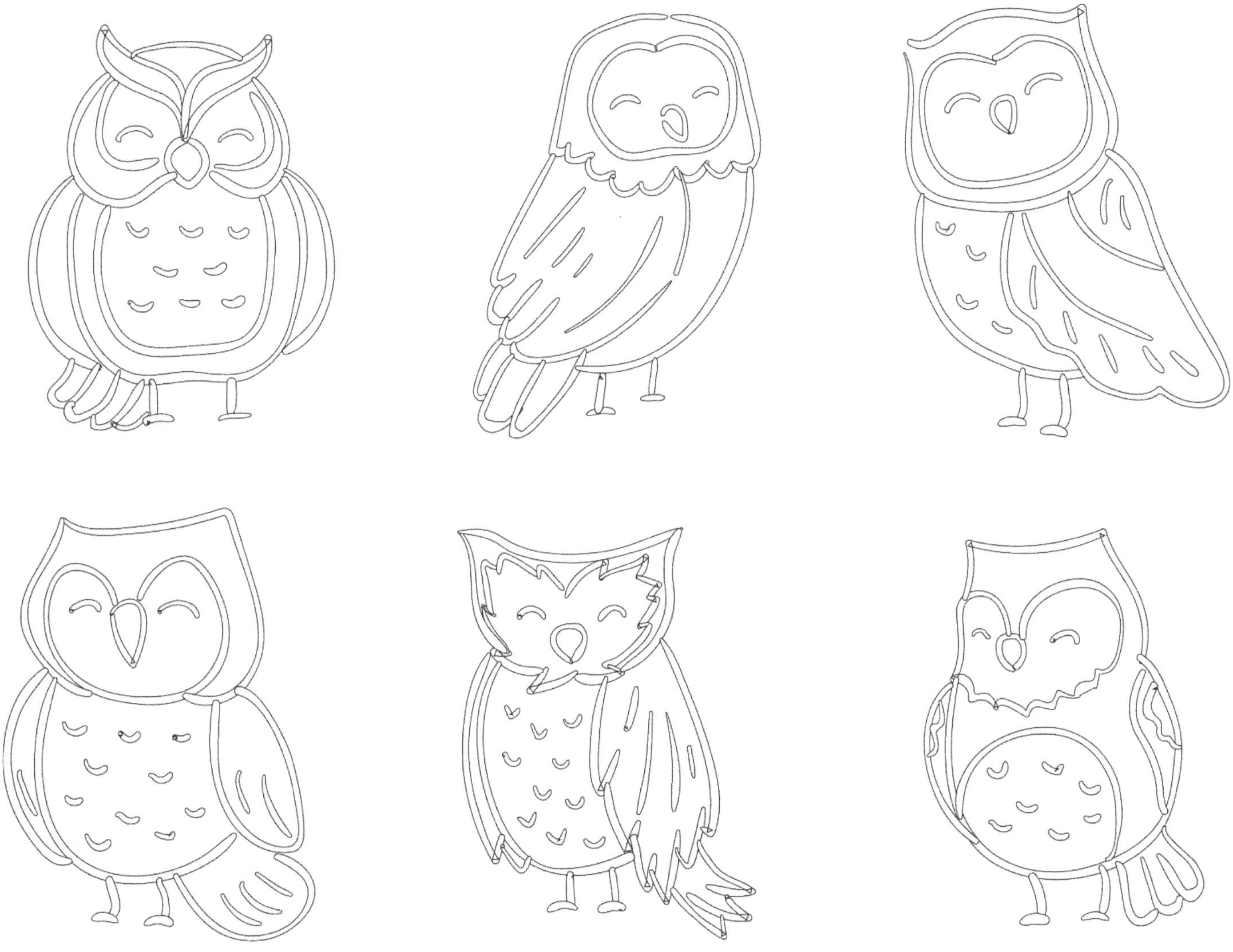

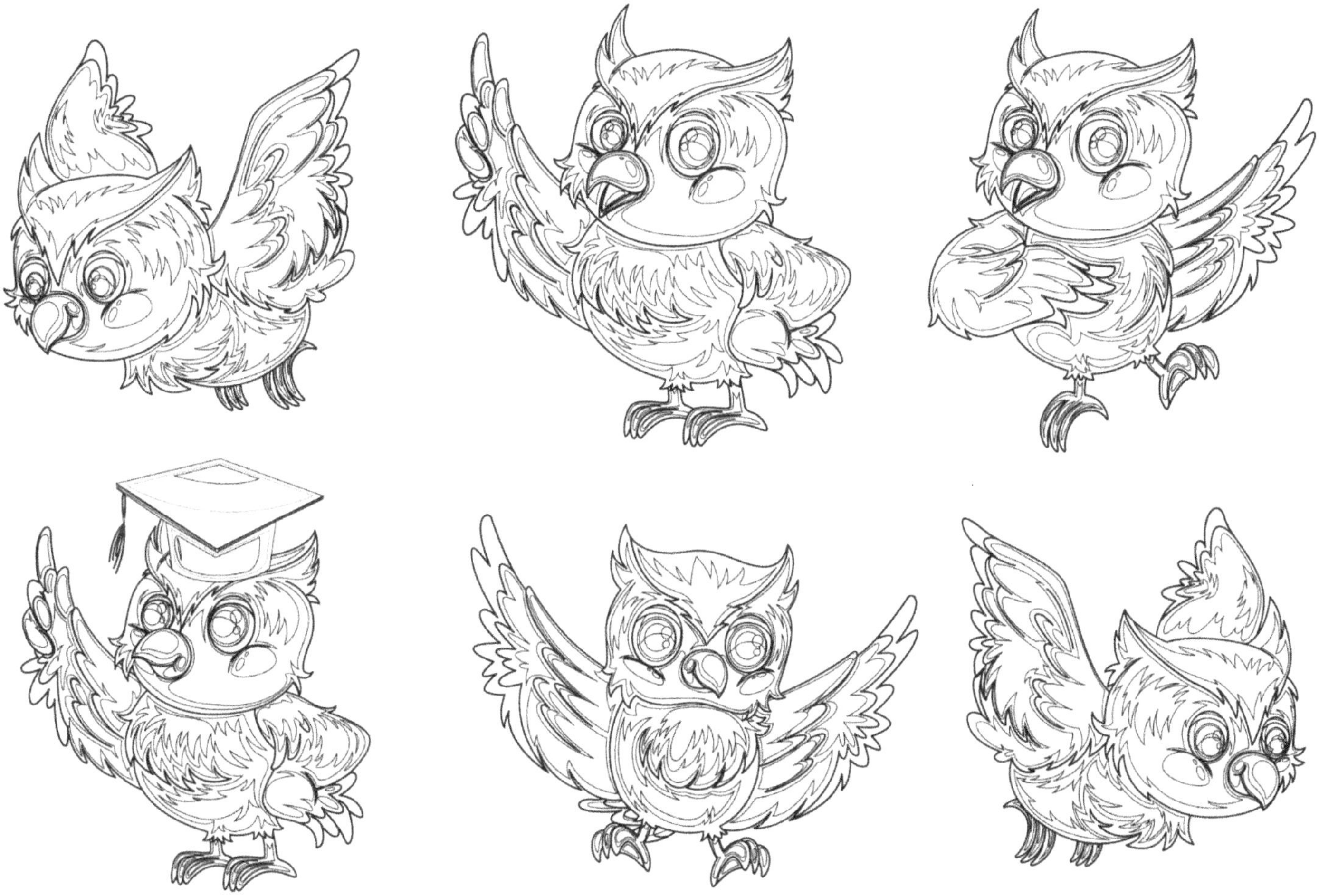

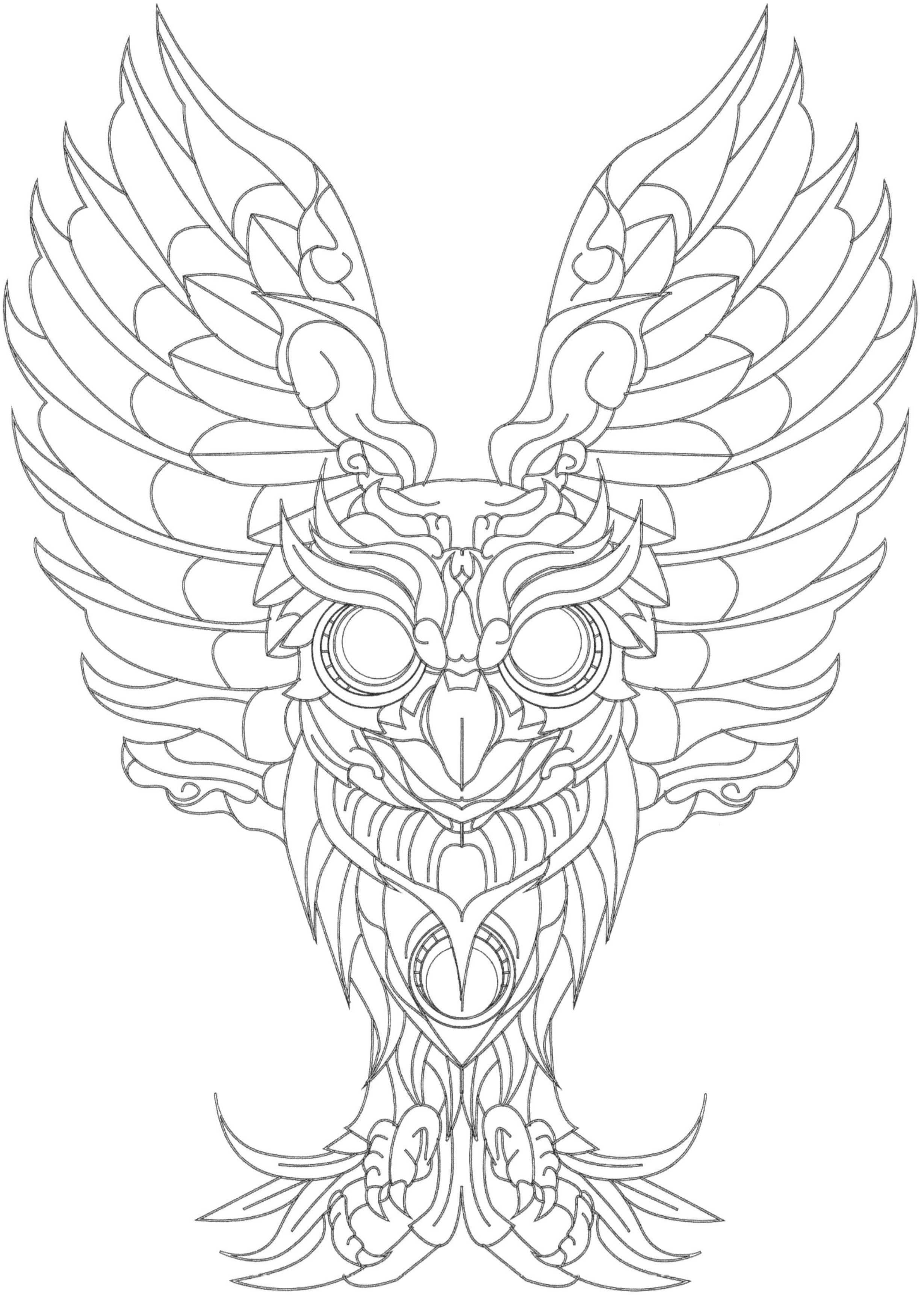

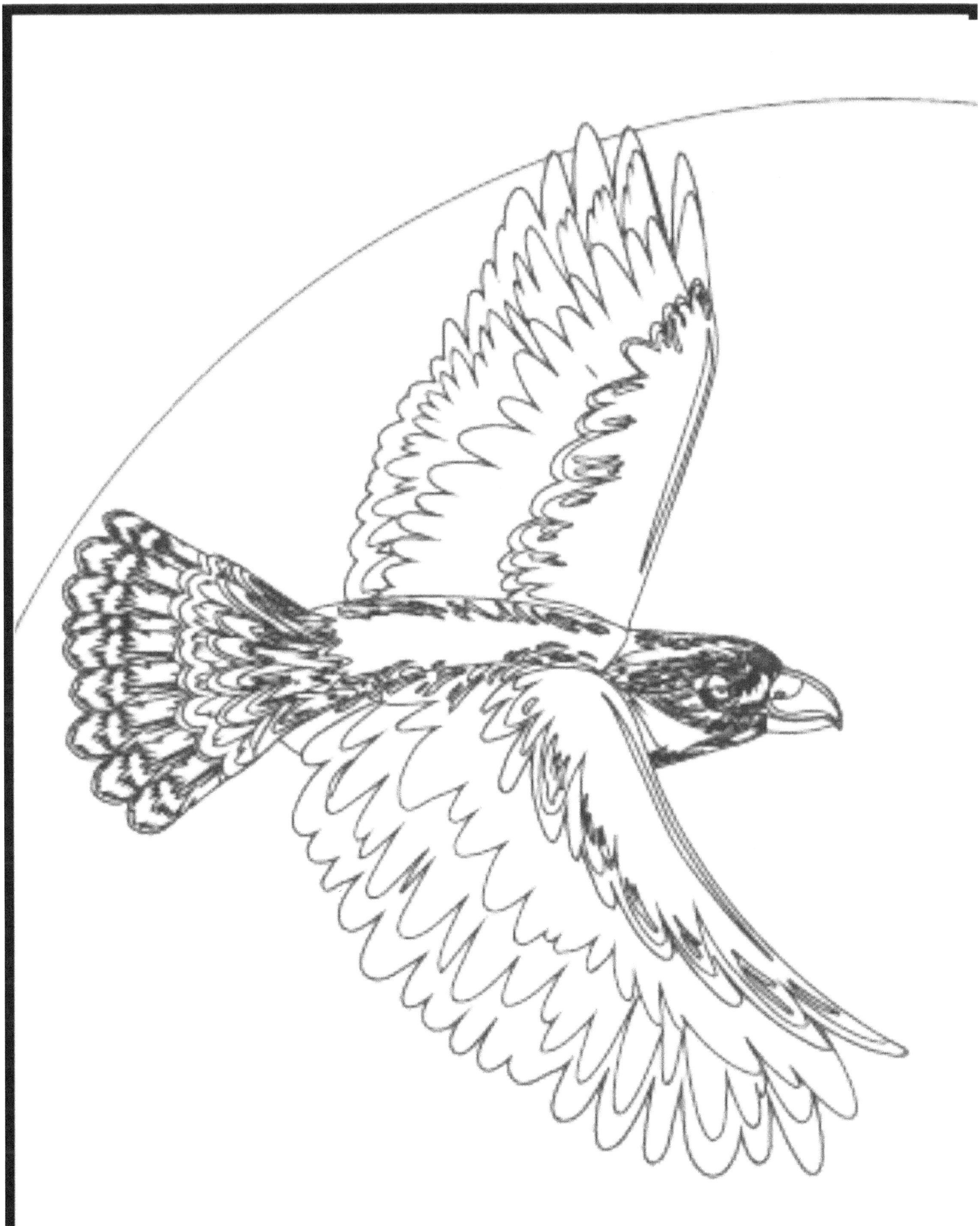

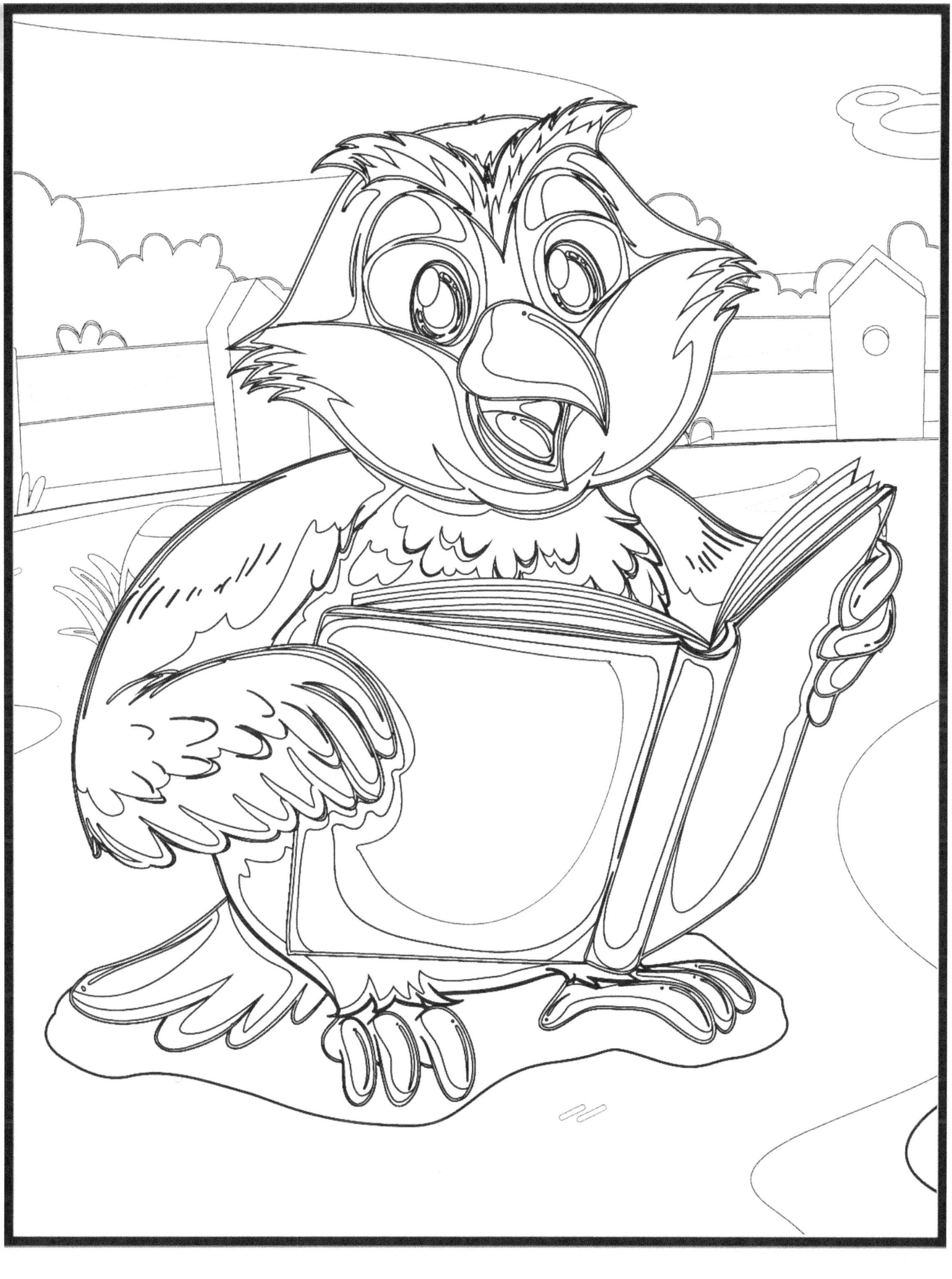

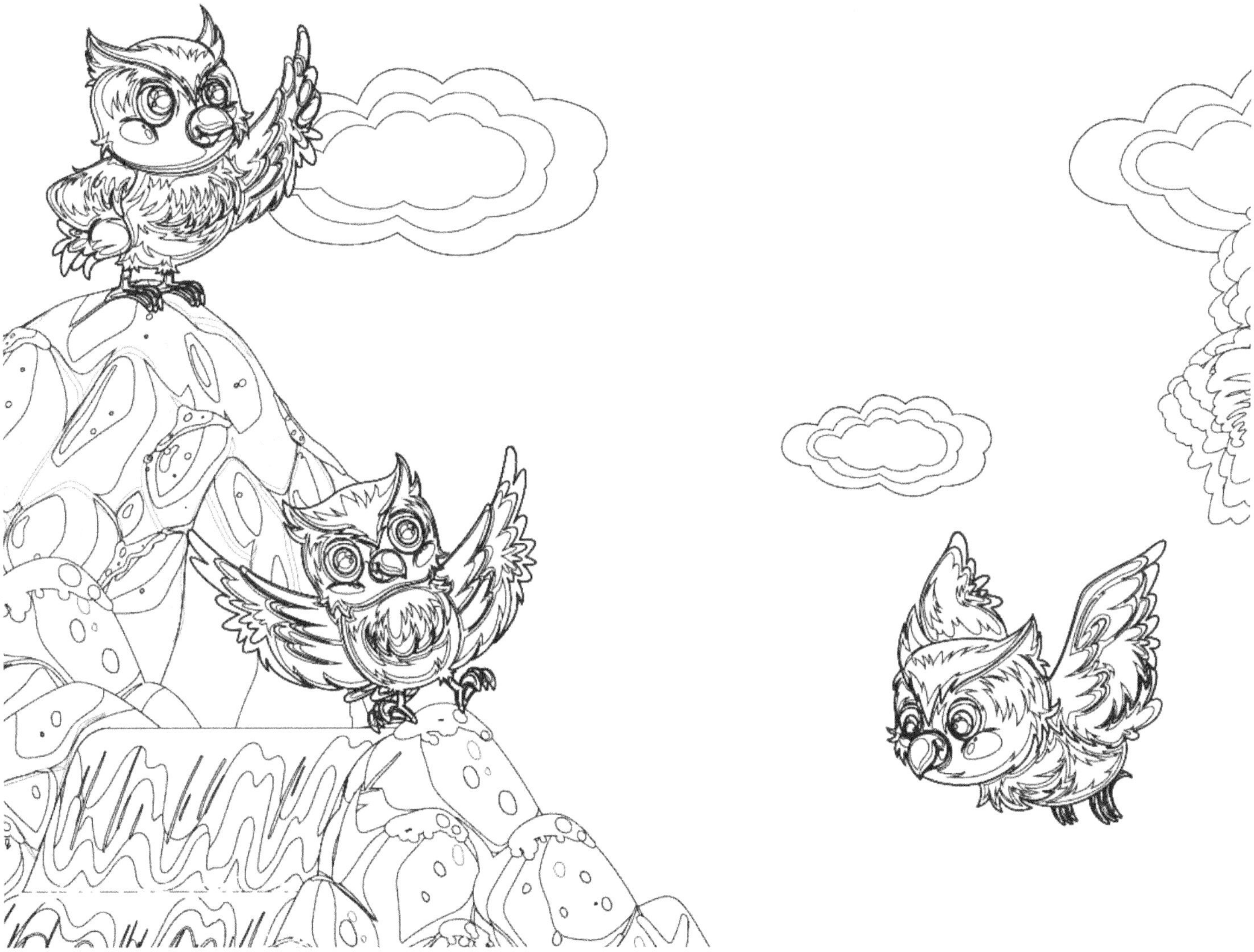

www.ingramcontent.com/pod-product-compliance
Lightning Source LLC
Chambersburg PA
CBHW081057240526
45465CB00025B/2570
*9798749756753*